sex
— and the —
PURSUIT
— of —
Chocolate

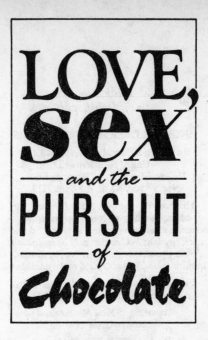

LOVE, SEX and the PURSUIT of Chocolate

NINA MYSKOW

with
Roslyn Grose

ANGUS
& ROBERTSON
PUBLISHERS

Dedication
To the Polish spirit

ANGUS & ROBERTSON PUBLISHERS

16 Golden Square, London W1R 4BN,
United Kingdom and
Unit 4, Eden Park, 31 Waterloo Road,
North Ryde, NSW, Australia 2113.

First published in the United Kingdom by
Angus & Robertson (UK) in 1990

Copyright © Nina Myskow and
Roslyn Grose 1990

Photographs © Nina Myskow,
Rex Features 1990

Typeset in Great Britain by The Wordshop,
Rossendale, Lancs.

Printed in Finland.

British Library Cataloguing in Publication Data
Myskow, Nina
Love, sex and the pursuit of chocolate.
1. Great Britain. Television programmes.
Criticism.
Biographies
I. Title II. Grose, Roslyn
791.45'092'4

ISBN 0 207 16606 4

Contents

Love, sex and the pursuit of chocolate

When I was a small child my father used to take me out attached to a little set of reins. Some people think I should still be wearing them.

I'm told by some friends that I make them feel safe – not because of the cuddly, nurturing side of my nature but because I can always be relied on to behave worse than they do. A night out with me, they say, is like having ringside seats at the ladies' mud wrestling – you can't quite bring yourself to look at what's happening in front of you. And you hope none of it will rub off.

It must have taken me the longest of anyone in the world to learn the blindingly obvious: life's too short (and so is my good friend Lynsey de Paul). That's why, at forty-four, I'm doing things I should have done when I was much younger.

Other people have blissful childhoods, wild youths and early burn-out, but my life has gone in reverse. I had a fairly boring childhood, a pleasantly dull youth and have only learned to go for the burn since turning forty. I'm having my wild youth (or lots of them, if you're talking toyboys) right now.

Blissfully, I only remember the good bits of my immediate past. Not because my mind always registers oblivion on the morning-after scale, but because, to me, there are only good bits.

I've never regretted anything. You can't change it once

you've done it. You can't go back and do it again another way.

People say to me '*Oh, God, do you actually sleep with someone the first night?*' Well, yeah, I could walk out the next day and get hit by a truck and I'd have missed out. Maybe it's not the beginning of a beautiful relationship, maybe you'll never see him again or maybe you will and it will be a disaster. But if that night was fine, that's what matters to me. I'd rather experience it than reject the whole event.

Forty was what did it, being forty and fat. I sat on a beach in Guadeloupe, lucky enough to be in such a beautiful place – but unhappy because I was too fat to feel happy there.

Inside myself I was a different person but I was too fat to have the confidence to be that person. I had learned to overcome it by talking and being entertaining but when it came down to it and however brave I was about it, however good at my job, I wasn't the person I wanted to be.

I thought I should go away and lose weight and come back and do this holiday again. I'd show them all. But then I realised that was wrong. Life is not a dress rehearsal. This moment would never come back.

I realised I didn't have time to waste any more. As a TV critic, I sat alone on a sofa for forty hours a week watching the box. But I wanted to go out, have dinner with people, go the movies, have fun. I realised I had to change the way I lived, the way I was physically and the way I worked.

Conning other people into thinking you are amazingly confident has always been easy. It's convincing yourself that's the hard part. I've never been backward about jumping in feet first. I've always jumped in and gone for it – and frequently found myself up to the ankle-straps in shit. But I've never not tried.

'Would you like to dive thirty feet on to a sponge?'

'Yeah, I'll try it. Give me another bottle of champagne

2

and I'll try anything.'

You can probably blame it all on my Polish-Scottish background. My father was in the Polish cavalry and came to Britain four days after Dunkirk. He was stationed in the north-east of Scotland where he met my mother, a university student doing biology. They were married in 1946 after he'd graduated from Edinburgh University. He knew he couldn't go back to Poland because the city of Lvov, where he came from, had become part of Russia.

It fills me with horror to think that if he'd gone back, I'd be Russian. Okay, so I've heard all the Polish jokes and maybe you think I *am* a Polish joke but I'd still rather be a Pole (preferably a bean-Pole). I think it's because they're always fun and get pissed and fall over and are rather smart. Having a good time is top priority.

When I was eighteen months old, we moved to South Africa where my father worked in forestry. But sadly he died when I was twelve and three years later we returned to Scotland to live with my grandfather.

From the sunshine and far horizons of Pietermaritzburg we moved into the little village of Wormit-on-Tay, overlooking the River Tay with Dundee on the other side. We looked across to the lights of Dundee – that city's best view, I can tell you.

It was very pretty – and freezing cold. Everything seemed grey and cold and narrow and small: the houses and the minds. The first Sunday there, I put on a pair of tight red jeans and my mother said, 'Oh, you can't wear those on a Sunday'. And I thought, what *have* I come to?

I spent the next seventeen years trying to escape and for a long time after I did get out, I felt physical terror of going back. If I heard a Scots accent I'd jump three feet. But I've come round from that. At least I love Billy Connolly – it's the tartan and bagpipes that give me a pain in the sporran.

Ever since I headed south to become first the *Sun*'s rock writer then the *News of the World*'s TV critic, I've been gradually rebuilding my life, making it the way I want it to be. I've reinvented myself. You may call me Nasty Nina, the Bitch on the Box, the Pink Blancmange or any other endearment that comes to mind and I'll be happy with that.

Now I've learned to grab life (and a few other bits) with both hands, there's no holding me (unless you're young, male and cute and your mother's not around). For the past three years I've been catching up on lost time and I never want to stop.

Now I'm horrified by people who have wasted their lives. One of my dearest friends lives very happily in the country. When I stay with her, she goes down to the Women's Institute for eggs and we queue up outside a scout hut with all the pensioners – and to me, it's like looking into the jaws of death. Not that I'm ageist but, is that what life is about? Pottering about buying plants, with all these old people elbowing other wrinklies out of the way?

It makes me think, 'this is not what I want, this is not life'. It may be some people's routine, it may be contentment but to me it's terrifying. I'm not saying don't buy your eggs at the WI, but to me that kind of existence signifies the acceptance of a dwindling spirit. When that thought first hit me, I jumped on a plane out of the country at three hours' notice, if only to prove to myself I wasn't in a rut.

I think there are signposts in life that keep you sedated. As a child there are Christmases, birthdays, school holidays and New Year resolutions. As an adult you go to work Monday to Friday, Friday night you go out, Saturday you go shopping, Sunday you have a big lunch. Housewives have Monday wash day, Tuesday ironing, a whole week of chores that keep them chained to the house. Everyone has patterns and habits that keep them tied to a boring existence.

Life can pass you by without your noticing. And suddenly you wake up in the Women's Institute elbowing

4

someone out of the way for cakes. Then suddenly everything is gone. You might have been married twenty-five years when your husband leaves you one morning for some bimbo who has bent over once too often by the filing cabinets. And there you are, grey hair, no waistline, no husband, nothing.

Complacency is the danger. Once you become complacent you might as well pull the duvet over your head. What's more, you'll probably find you're under it on your own.

The fear of getting stuck in a routine existence is why I always carry my passport in my handbag: it'll always get you further than a toothbrush and a pair of clean knickers. If you carry those as well, you really are ready for anything. It is also why I always wear shocking pink. I like to shock and I like to feel permanently in the pink.

Also, I am still getting my own back on my mother for something that happened when I was five. She was going to make me an angora bolero, that ultimate fluffy Fifties garment for wearing over your party frock. I can remember standing in the department store and spotting this shocking pink angora I really wanted and my mother said no, it wasn't tasteful and it wasn't nice. She made me have a brownish amber instead.

When I got home I was so upset I went shaking with rage to our next-door neighbour and said, 'Look what she's made me buy, look what she's making me wear'.

She also made me wear brown Clarks sandals. I was so ashamed of still having to wear them when I was twelve. I remember standing at a bus stop waiting to go shopping when I realised my classmates could see me from a window across the road. I was so mortified I put the shopping basket over my shoes and prayed for the bus to come. That is why I never wear anything but silly shoes. Best of all, shocking pink silly shoes – and try saying that after a few champagne cocktails.

Now I'm not suggesting that you should all rush off to Pied a Terre pronto, buy some pavement-puncturing heels and you too could end up on 'New Faces' or standing in for Derek Jameson (who needs a New Face more than most).

But there is infinitely more to life than painting yourself pink.

'What? What?' I hear you pant impatiently.

Well, there is chocolate. And the thrill of spending money you don't have. And behaving badly in your best clothes. And never, ever, doing housework. And having more holidays than Fergie. And chocolate. And telling people what you really think. And being friends with Elton John. And buying size 12 clothes. And fitting into them. And pink champagne. And chocolate.

All this and more can be yours.

On the other hand there are a lot of nice people waiting for you down at the Women's Institute.

Chocs away

My mother has a photo of me aged eighteen months on top of the piano at home and I look like a lump of dough in a petticoat. I'm amazed the whole photograph doesn't crash through the piano.

I asked my mother once how she let me get like that and she said, 'Because you were such a greedy baby.' Then she told me it was the only way she could stop me crying, by stuffing some food into my mouth. Thanks Mum.

But be that as it may, I have always found food a great solace and therefore a huge problem. I can look down and see it's a huge problem. All that school food that other people hated – like spotted dick and runny custard – well, I loved it and always wanted seconds. I've always adored stodgy things (no, not you, Bernard Manning). When we moved back to Scotland there was always high tea at five o'clock – bacon and eggs plus cream cakes. Imagine what that does to you.

As a teenager I wasn't hugely fat, but I was always plump. The fact that I never did any exercise didn't help, either. I hated anything athletic – I was always the one standing crying on the side or shoved off the end of the diving board. I was so awful at tennis that I remember my gym teacher sending twenty balls to me to hit and when she got to the twentieth ball she just slammed it straight at me. I could understand why she was angry: I

7

was even too clumsy to be a ball-girl without getting in everyone's way.

By the time I grew up I was so into food I couldn't pass a cake shop. As for biscuits, I could eat a whole packet in one go – then I'd feel so guilty I'd hide the wrapper under the bed.

I was never happy with myself – I never felt right sitting, standing or walking. I always felt self-conscious and always had to make up for it with the old verbals, trying to be funny.

Being overweight is a great excuse: you can tell yourself that if you were thinner everything would be okay. You can blame everything that goes wrong in your life on your size. You choose to ignore the fact that you *can* do something about it.

Not that, in company with most of the women in Britain, I didn't try. Over the years I've been on every kind of diet: the Mayo Clinic one with all the eggs (farted a lot, didn't lose weight); a milk and egg diet; even a total three-week fast – I lost a stone and a half on nothing but water. But my head was so light I had to tie it down.

I went to Weight Watchers too but they were obsessed with elephants and, I'm sorry, I don't want to identify with people who are six stone overweight. Of course they are the ones who are most successful because they can lose the most weight in a week. But that was just depressing for the rest of us who only needed to lose a stone or two.

About the only diet I have never tried is the Junk Food Diet which implied you could practically live in MacDonalds and come out thin. The trouble with that one was that it would work for anyone who could control their eating. For somebody like me, with no control, once you passed through the portals of MacDonalds, the gate to the sty, you would stick your nose in the trough. It was a licence to swill.

The most successful diet I ever went on was a high-protein regime of meat and citrus fruit, no vegetables.

8

But the fat burning off gave you such raging halitosis you could hire yourself out as a paint-stripper! It was also terribly dangerous because it wasted heart muscle – but it worked. Only the fear of ending up both thin and dead stopped me following that one again.

Dieters get to know the ins-and-outs of their bodies as intimately as car maniacs know the working of their motors. And can be just as boring about them. You know when you're losing weight: bad breath. You know when you need to slam protein in to wake up your metabolism: most fat people have been dead for years. You know the calorie count of everything; you know the fat content and the fibre content.

But I'm one of those people who can hardly eat anything and *still* not lose weight. Nobody ever believes you aren't cheating, which is even more discouraging.

Being a chocaholic has never helped. I know every twenty-four-hour petrol station within a ten-mile radius of where I live – because when you have an insatiable craving for chocolate at 3 a.m. that's the only place you'll find it. David Attenborough once told me he was passionate about Mars Bars. But that's not a real chocaholic to me, too much gunge and not enough chocolate – even though he says he can eat three in one go.

When I was first dieting properly I had to have, every week, one white fresh cream Belgian chocolate and it used to be coffee flavoured with walnut. I bought them one at a time from Harvey Nichols at 30p to 40p each, depending on the weight. I always *prayed* for one of the heavier ones. I used to go in every Monday and ask for one. After about six weeks they said, 'Why do you always ask for *one*?' I said it was because I was on a diet. And because I was a chocaholic, I had to have just one, otherwise temptation would get the better of me. After that, they wouldn't sell me any more even when I asked.

My other piece of discipline was that I wouldn't eat it till I was in the car park. My sprint from the chocolate counter through the men's department and out the door would have made even Flo Jo lose her breath.

Selfridges had a promotion once when you could pay £2.50 to go to the store and eat as many chocolates as you liked. I didn't go near the West End for a whole week. They say there are only a certain amount of chocolates you can eat – but not me, I can go on forever.

As a professional dieter for years, I couldn't have any food in the fridge at all because I would just open the door and – whoomf – I'd scoff the lot. I had all the control of a perished panty-girdle.

One time I woke in the middle of the night feeling hungry and I knew I had flour, some butter, an egg and some jam. I would make scones, which are dead fast. I felt like the old Joan Rivers joke about Elizabeth Taylor standing in front of the microwave and shouting 'Hurry!'

I could barely wait the ten minutes for the scones to cook. It was about three in the morning and I burned my lips, I was so anxious to eat them. I slammed them in one after the other and by the time I'd eaten seven I felt so guilty and really disgusting. I thought to myself, 'I'll throw the rest of them in the bin, at least I haven't eaten all of them'.

I did just that. And then I thought, 'When you get up in the morning, you will get them out of the bin. So make yourself a cup of tea then throw the used teabag on top of them.'

When I got up in the morning I thought, '*Oh no*, you made scones in the middle of the night, how disgusting.' Then, 'Well, at least you didn't eat all of them, you only ate seven.' Then, while I was making coffee, 'I wonder if the teabag hit the scones?' Next thing, I took the lid off the bin, put my head in the bin and picked out the four scones which didn't get hit *out of the rubbish bin*. Then I *ATE* four scones which had been lying in a filthy rubbish bin all night.

I have also got up in the middle of the night to make rice pudding. Now that takes perseverance because it takes at least an hour and a half. And every twenty minutes you have to stir it to get the skin right!

It's always stodgy things you lust after in the middle of the night. Like donuts. I have a favourite deli up the hill where I used to go on Sunday mornings because Michael Palin and Jonathan Miller go there and I used to lurk around because I love Michael Palin. Well, they make these lovely big yellowy donuts with jam in the middle. They are just the most gorgeous things. I bought one once on a cold Sunday and from then on I was hooked. I could eat three at a time. I thought it was just because they were great donuts. Honestly, I might as well have bought a gross of them and just strapped them round my waist and let them dangle down my thighs. Plus a few to hang around my cheeks and under my chin.

One Sunday evening just after 'Spitting Image' I remember thinking to myself, 'Gotta have donuts'. The shop might be shut, there was snow on the ground and I had to have donuts. I kept saying to myself, 'You're surely not going to go out? In your gloves, your boots?' Was this the depth to which I'd sunk? I told myself that perhaps I could buy some apples . . . As I put my coat on I was saying, 'You're not really doing this? I can't believe you're doing this.'

It took me five minutes to start the car, it was so cold. When I got to the shop there was no fresh bread, nothing. But I told myself I was there to buy apples and I did buy apples. But as I was going past the freezer I thought I'd just stick my head in and look. And there was a Sweet Trolley thing of three long donuts. I took it out and read the packet: defrost for one hour. An hour! It was already 11 p.m.

Know what I did? I turned the central heating up, put them on a towel on a radiator in the bathroom and they defrosted in forty minutes. I ate the first one and it was disgusting, and the second one just to make sure. Then I ate the third one. And then I almost ate the box as well.

One of my worst excesses was with Chicken MacNug-

gets, which I decided to have because they're less fatten-
ing than a Big Mac. They come in packs of six, nine or
twenty and by the time I got into MacDonalds, I could
hear myself asking for twenty. Now what do those spotty
assistants care what you order? Yet I felt obliged to make
clear that it wasn't just for one. So I ordered two large
things of chips, two milkshakes and two apple pies. And I
ate one Big Mac and French fries, one milkshake and one
apple pie in the car on the way home. After which I sat
down and ate the *other* whole meal.

I *never* get sick of food. I can *always* eat chocolate
Hobnobs or Marie biscuits stuck together with butter. . . . The other thing I always dream about when I am
on a diet is peanut butter and golden syrup sandwiches.
It is the most delicious amalgam, it doesn't stick to the
roof of your mouth and on flabby bread it is just fantastic.
When you add sliced bananas to this, or crunchy bacon,
it is out of this world. But I have to remind myself that in
the year before his death, Elvis Presley lived on peanut
butter and jelly sandwiches *fried in butter*. I've never gone
that far but on the other hand I've thought, 'I understand
this boy.'

I now control my eating by way of The Diet Police,
imaginary monsters invented by a man I know – every
time I think about food, they mentally raid me. And I
have a pig in the fridge that goes 'oink, oink' whenever
the door opens – that is the police siren. I tell it to shut up
occasionally – but I think perhaps there should be real
diet police to arrest you and stop you pigging out. After
all, you can get arrested for drinking too much.

It's only in the past three years that I have learned to
control my eating. Now I want to help everyone else who
is having problems to do it too. If I can beat the bulge,
anybody can. I'm like a reformed smoker. I want to
convey to people how much happier they'll be – but I
hear all the same excuses coming out, like 'I'll start on
Monday' or 'I'm too tired' or 'I'm too weak-willed' or

12

'I'm not fat, it's all water-retention' – all the boring things I used to say. That's then followed by 'I can't exercise, I've got a bad back'. Well, I know exercise is boring when you've got all these bits wobbling around you. But it makes life so much more pleasant when you don't have to cringe when you're walking down the street and catch sight of yourself in a shop window – something I used to do all the time.

You can't get away from fat, it's always there, hanging in lumps under your arm. Even when you're sitting down, you're hanging all over the chair. When you cross your legs you can feel it. When you sit down you can feel yourself squidging all the way down. And when you feel your clothes are too tight, something makes you want to eat more because you hate yourself so much.

I have a pair of pale pink jeans which I bought when I was slender-ish and two summers ago I couldn't get them past my knees. They are a tight size 12 and they are the way I can always tell if I am thinner or fatter.

I have never owned a pair of blue jeans because a) I hate blue and b) I was never the right shape to wear them. I was always encased in fat, like a fly encased in amber, only that sounds too attractive.

The trouble with jeans is that to get into them you have to pull them on, do the button up then lie on the floor and pull the zip up with the help of a coat hanger. Well, zips aren't designed to be pulled up by coat hangers any more. You have to use pliers. But pliers cut your hands, so you have to put a glove on and lie on the floor and heave, trying not to get the flesh caught in the zip. Then you lever yourself up and look in the mirror and notice the overhang at the waist and you think, never mind, I've done them up. Then you let out a sigh of relief – and the whole thing explodes apart again. If you could only lie there and have the fat massaged away from you.

My rock bottom moment was when a toyboy I'd been out with turned me over in *News of the World*. Being described as a 'great white naked whale' to 15 million

13

people doesn't do a lot for your morale, I promise. It is the biggest-ever incentive to diet.

When you're a teenager you all pile into chaps' cars but you can never sit on anyone's knee. Or if you do you have to hang on to the strap so you can redistribute the weight. That's why I could never fancy anyone who was fat because people would think, 'Oh she's fat, so all she could get was somebody fat.' And you could hear them thinking, 'No wonder they're fat, they probably lock themselves away and stuff themselves.'

I am now the slimmest I've been in the last decade. And it's all thanks to Jane Fonda, whose exercises I do religiously and Club Med, whose holidays made me want to get sleek enough to enjoy them even more.

When I did the first series of 'New Faces' I spent the whole fee for the series on a Club Med holiday in Guadeloupe. I was eleven and a half stone, five-foot-two and a half – and unhappy. I'd just celebrated my birthday, which was when it really hit home that I had reached forty and my hips had reached further than that. (When your hips are bigger than your age, you've really got a problem.)

There is nothing more upsetting then being on a beach with hundreds of marvellous French women who look good because they work at it. British bodies are on the whole appalling: the paleness, the doughiness, the unliving flesh. Disgusting. Pick up any French magazine and there are ads for anti-cellulite products. Yet here you can go to your doctor and he will tell you there is no such thing. But I can look down and *see it*. Some people say you should make a feature of cellulite and stick sequins in your dimples but I think that's accepting yourself a little too much. The French are brought up to use creams and scrub themselves and you look at them on the beach and it works. They don't have cellulite because they know that it exists. We say it doesn't exist and we have it – now that's completely Irish to me!

There's nothing worse than going on holiday, fat. When sarongs and pareos were in it was okay-ish – you could wrap yourself up in one and sling it low to show off your boobs. Then you could surreptitiously slip it off and lie flat on your beach mat without looking too bad. Lying on your stomach, you could look more or less okay. But then came the time you got too hot and had to go in the sea or the pool. There's no way to do it with your body in a flattering position – unless you could walk like a crab, still lying down. So you lie there thinking about it all the time, do you go for a swim when everybody else is at lunch? Do you just decide not to care? In the meantime, you are at least getting brown and on the plus side, a suntan is slimming. Big brown wobbly thighs are some-how more attractive than big white wobbly thighs.

As a fatty, you can divide the world into fat people and thin people – and you've got nothing in common with thin people. I once went to France with a girl I knew. As we drove to Dover in my car, she bought a bag of Cadbury's Roses and I thought, she must care nothing about chocolates because they're horrible granny's choco-lates. She offered me one, she had one then she put the bag away. I thought, well, I don't like them but I'll eat them – but she put them away and didn't offer them again. Then four days later, on the boat on the way back, she took them out of her handbag again. And she hadn't touched them since we left! Well, I'm sorry, I couldn't be friendly with anyone like that. There was no way we had anything in common. How can you operate like that, with such ghastly self-control?

There are people around who say you shouldn't worry about weight, you should be happy as you are, and what I say to that is, 'Bollocks!' Only thin people say that, of course, people like Selina Scott. It makes you want to punch them in the mouth.

I get annoyed when thin people won't let themselves have something that I want to have: they *can* have it but they don't. Like a pudding. Sometimes there's a terrific pudding and you can see all the fat people round the table desperate to have it – but they won't have it. And the thin people *could* have it but *they* won't have it, either.

It's a funny thing that when you're fat you have to be terribly nice to people. You have to apologise for being fat so you're terribly nice all the time. Therefore one good reason to get thin is so you can be really foul to people – and nobody can shout back, 'You fat cow.' Think of all the skinny bitches you can carve up. . . .

When you're fat, your whole life is engulfed by it. You sit on beaches looking for people fatter than you. When you're with a group of people you ask yourself, 'Am I the fattest person here?'

Your fat is there when you're trying clothes on, walking about, sitting. You feel clumsy and not like one of the human race. You feel you're in a minority when in fact you're in the majority.

So why do we all try to diet? You may say it's for other people, that you've got a terrific boyfriend or you want to find a terrific boyfriend, lover or husband. But in fact it doesn't matter a toss to anybody else whether you're fat or thin. The only person worth dieting for is YOU. People think it's selfish to look after Number One but unless you do that you can't begin to relate to other people.

We are all driven to diet for different personal reasons, like taking your clothes off and looking at yourself; or having someone else take your clothes off and look at you; or being described in a national newspaper as a 'great white naked whale.'

Revenge is another strong spur and succeeding is the greatest revenge of all. There is nothing like the joy of seeing some skinny bitch who's always patronised you and hearing her say, 'Ooh, you're looking well.' She has to say something, she can't ignore the fact that you've lost a lot of weight.

One sure way to make yourself diet is to look at yourself in the mirror while you're eating. It can put you off for days. Another time to start dieting is when someone has just fallen out of love with you. The most obvious thing to do at a time like this is to stick your head in the biscuit tin and graze. But this is one time you ought to take a grip of yourself otherwise your clothes will grip YOU so tight they'll strangle you.

Control over your private eating is the hardest thing to achieve. Most people can do it in public – not eating bread, potatoes, chips, sweet things when they're out. But when they go home they empty the fridge. That's why I keep nothing in the fridge, except for low-calorie yoghurts, Diet Coke and salads.

As far as cakes go, the only way to deal with them is with bad behaviour. It is better to throw cakes than to eat them. Heave all those calories over someone else. Then you apologise, 'Please let me lick – I mean clean – that off!'

Whenever I'm on a diet I read recipe books as keenly as a dirty old man devours pornography. I read all the ingredients: pasta, cream, eggs . . . by the time I get to the bacon I'm practically salivating. I also make cakes for other people: unbirthday cakes, hello and goodbye cakes. But whenever I'm tempted to dip my finger in the mixture and have a taste I think of a story I once read about a woman who was using her mixer. She held up the blades to have a lick, accidentally pushed the button and cut off her tongue. It shocks me back to my diet every time.

What we all need are ways to prevent us eating at the very moment when we are about to take a bite. Here's one that never fails for me: as you open your mouth and are about to take a big bite of a chocolate eclair or a donut or a Big Mac and chips plus strawberry milkshake and apple pie – imagine yourself French-kissing Derek Jameson!

If that doesn't make you choke on your first French fry, here are some other off-putters: when you're standing in the cinema about to buy a big thing of Butterkist popcorn and chocolate peanuts plus Diet Coke, imagine yourself standing there naked.

OR, if you've started doing aerobics or exercise class, just as you're about to reach out for that ice-cream, concentrate on how you felt at the end of your last exercise session, that utter exhaustion. Did you go through all that hard work for nothing?

OR conjure up the face of someone you fancy looking at you with an expression of disgust and horror at the sight of your wobbliest bits – an expression along the lines of Harrison Ford's when he saw the pit of writhing snakes in *Raiders of the Lost Ark*. Or Woody Allen's when he feared he might be crushed by the giant boob in *Everything You Always Wanted to Know About Sex*.

You might also like to picture yourself in an Azzeldine Alaia frock, one of those black bandage numbers that make model girls look like goddesses but make you look like the Michelin man.

I've found that such off-putting fantasies don't half stamp out your hunger. My head is now so full of them that I can do a slow cruise of the most sumptuous buffet – and come away with a plate piled high with salad. I've learned to love things I never thought of swallowing before, like salads and grilled fish and diet drinks and black coffees.

I've learned just to look at delicacies like profiteroles, vol-au-vents, petits fours and rum truffles without automatically reaching out for one. I have learned from bitter experience that one is not enough – and if I scoff six I'll be back in white whale territory.

Worst of all, I'll have to stop bitching and start being *nice* to people again.

Toyboys don't need jump leads

My first toyboy adventure was more rock 'n' roll than boy-meets-older-woman. I was in Newcastle a few years ago doing a live late-night Friday television show, and there was a rock band on. One of its members was a blond boy who came over to me and said, 'Hi, do you remember me?' We had met when I'd interviewed him years before when he was in another band, so we chatted away.

I was very tired and had to get a train early on the Saturday morning back to London. But when I got back to my hotel room he rang me there. 'Come to my room for a drink', he invited. I thanked him for the offer but refused. He persisted, 'Well, why don't I come up to your room?' I was either so stupid or so zonked that I didn't instantly realise what he had in mind. When it dawned on me, I thought it was quite unthinkable. I took the phone off the hook.

The lights were out and I had just dropped off to sleep when there was a thunderous knocking on the door. I didn't have a dressing gown so I wrapped the sheet around me and went to answer it. He was standing there with a bottle of wine, two glasses and a plastic flower between his teeth.

This was when I thought: fine, okay, you win. And it was great fun. But I thought of it as a one-off, an isolated incident. He must have been in his early twenties and I thought of it as just one of those rock 'n' roll events.

The next time was on holiday in Turkey, where I spent a week at a Club Med. Every night at the nightclub where everyone was leaping around the floor, there was this noticeably attractive, really nice Belgian guy. I know nice Belgian sounds like a contradiction in terms: they are so boring as a race they usually try to convince you they're wacky, 'Hello, I'm Belgian, I'm wacky. Look I'm a crazy person.' But this guy was different.

He was twenty-one, his name was Peter, he spoke very good English and he was a philosophy and politics student at Brussels University – about six feet tall with lovely blond, sticky-up, hedgehog hair. He was on his own and whenever I started to leap around, he always used to come and dance with me. We started to talk to each other on the beach, but I just thought he was a cute kid. He made me laugh and I made him laugh. However, on the fourth night we were dancing away and there was a slow dance and he was suddenly dancing very close. I thought, 'Hang on, what's going on here?'

I remember arguing with him and saying, 'Look, I'm forty-one years old.' But he wouldn't listen, he just said, 'Who's counting?' So I dragged him over to what light there was and made him look closely at me. 'Look at the wrinkles', I ordered. (I'm not sure why I tried to talk him out of it but I didn't want to wake up in the morning and hear him say, 'Christ, what have I done?') So I made him look at the wrinkles. All he said was, 'I don't see any wrinkles.'

I asked him, 'What do you want to be when you grow up?' and he said he wanted to be a diplomat. I told him he obviously had a brilliant career as a diplomat ahead of him. He denied that diplomacy had anything to do with what he felt – so from that moment we just had a wonderful time. We slept together that night and I remember thinking it would be a one-night affair and really embarrassing – next day he would do the old eye-swerve and walk right past me. I braced myself for that. But it didn't happen at all, he was really so sweet. He came tearing round to look for me but was quite happy to do whatever I wanted to do. He would just appear and ask if I'd like a drink. Or he'd come up and clean my sunglasses for me: maybe he was used to doing it for his mum or something?

When I got home, there was a message on my answering machine saying how much he missed me and I got a postcard from him as well. I didn't respond but I thought, 'This is all right.'

What was quite extraordinary to me was the thought that it's easy to pull someone if you're dressed up and looking good, tarted up to the nines and terribly sophisticated – by this I mean looking the best you can. But I always imagined that when you're slobbing around on a beach with your hair all scraped back and sea water in your eyes, any man would find you about as desirable as a sea-slug. This doesn't seem to be so at all.

When the whole toyboy thing started, no one was more staggered than me. It was just a bonus, not something I had gone looking for. It just happened and I found it very bizarre – lovely, but bizarre.

Since then, I've only been out with one older man. The third time we went out I climbed into his car and he said, 'Good God, a skirt!'

'What do you mean?'

'You always wear trousers!'

I pointed out, that this was only the third time we'd seen each other. He wouldn't let it go, though. He clearly thought two-thirds of your time in trousers was a poor show. I felt warning bells ring. He was starting to bristle and I could sense trouble.

We had been introduced by a very warm and witty career woman whom he had known for years. And we were discussing how bright and clever and successful she was, when he said, 'She's just a bit too feminist for my liking.'

I asked what he meant by that, and he said, 'Well,

21

she's a bit unfeminine.'

I felt furious. 'How dare you say that? The only thing that will excuse you is your age and your upbringing,' I added insult value with, 'That's why I like younger men: they've been brought up by women who think like me. You haven't had that advantage.' He didn't pursue that angle any further.

He was the sort of man who always raced to open doors for you and displayed a lot of old-fashioned Good Manners – but it was a bit like being out with your father.

When it comes to sex – and it always does – I have developed an infinite preference for young men. With middle-aged men I've come to the conclusion that those who can't get it up are the ones who try hardest to put women down. Young men don't seem to have that problem. But that's not the only reason I go out with younger men or how I got my reputation as a toyboy fancier. It is simply that when you're as incredibly old as I am, forty-four, *every* man is a toyboy.

Also, I've always had this thing about married men: I think they are absolutely Hands Off. That's because a) on the whole I like other women too much to do that to them and b) if a married man is going to cheat on his wife, he is ultimately going to cheat on you too.

I've seen too many friends sitting round on their own at weekends, on birthdays, at Christmas, crying and waiting for phone calls. Just when you need to be with somebody most, you're not. I don't know how you put up with that situation and the jealousy it brings. I suppose everyone has to make their own decision about whether this makes them happier than it makes them unhappy. There must be cases where two people do fall in love like this and eventually get together and it is obviously meant to be. But I wouldn't deliberately go into any relationship with a married man.

Single men my own age are rare beings and, with my reputation, you could hardly blame them for not thinking of me as their ideal date. I went out to dinner with one such gent just after the *News of the World* had published that kiss-and-tell story. As we walked into the smart north London restaurant we could see a couple of big tables obviously occupied by office celebrations or birthday parties: they were full of filing clerks with too much make-up and not enough brains. As I walked in I heard my name being whispered – we had to stand by them while we waited for a table and I could hear them talking. One girl suddenly said very loudly, 'Well, 'e don't look like much of a toyboy to me.'

I turned round and said, 'It's sad, really, how they age. He was when I took him out earlier.' The whole table burst out laughing – a joke has always been my best form of defence.

For instance I always try to get in the one about age first. The morning after one amorous adventure, sitting in a taxi with a guy in his dinner suit, I was putting on my make-up. 'You'd better look at this because this is the worst it is', I advised him. He just said, 'What *are* you talking about?' So I suppose I'm really aware of my wrinkles, though I don't much mind them – it's just that I'd rather mention them before anyone else does.

If a guy says, 'Christ, what's in that handbag, it weighs a ton?' I always say, 'Oh it's all make-up.' Or I warn them I'll probably be late turning up, 'It takes the putty longer to set at my age.' There's no point in pretending to myself that I look like an eighteen-year-old. I don't. On the other hand, I haven't got the brain of an eighteen-year-old, either.

I'm actually having to be very wary now. I can't just go round pulling nineteen-year-olds any more, having been so badly stitched up by one. In a way I understand the temptation – if they've never had any money in their lives, to be offered £2,000 by a newspaper is a trip to Australia or India for them.

People always ask me where I meet all these tasty young men. On dance floors, mostly, is the answer. You meet them wherever you can dance – and you certainly

do not meet them in the queue at Burger King at 3 a.m.
Nor should you pick them up in the homes of their
parents who happen to be your friends. There are rules *I*
wouldn't digress from and one is that I wouldn't seduce
the nineteen-year-old son of my best friend.

I met one of my favourite toyboys at a party after a record
industry awards ceremony where I'd gone in the hope of
meeting an ex-lover of mine. It was absolutely crammed
and people were throwing alcohol down their throats like
there was no tomorrow. As I trawled through the crowd I
became aware of two guys, a tall dark one and a slightly
smaller blond one. The tall one was saying, 'There's that
Nina Myskow from "New Faces" on telly.' And as I
passed, the blond one shouted, 'Way to go, Nina' – a very
silly American phrase which seems to mean something
like 'Good for you'.

I walked over to him and said, 'What do you mean?'

'Don't you remember us – we met at Cliff Richard's
funeral?'

Very funny. But he persisted, 'Don't you remember
us, Simon and Nigel.'

I replied rather rudely, 'Nobody's called Simon and
Nigel unless they're estate agents.' And their jaws dropped – that's exactly what they did for a living.

Having won that round, I went off to have a drink with
the man I'd originally come to see. But later as I passed
the other two they asked if I'd have a drink with them. I
did because I'll drink with anybody. They were being
very entertaining until two women arrived by their side
who were like every wife or girlfriend you ever see when
you're talking to their men: they had their hard eyes on
and they were looking daggers. I said how nice it was to
meet them, and offered to buy them all a drink, thinking,
'That'll be my debt repaid.' After that, we all said goodnight and parted.

However, as I left, the blond one followed me and
asked, 'When are we going to have dinner?' He was very

persistent, but when I said, 'Hadn't you better go back to your wife – or girlfriend,' he said she wasn't either. She was his ex-girlfriend. She had a head that was flat like a snake and proceeded to make a complete asp of herself. In the end she came stomping up to him screaming, 'If you don't leave that bitch alone I'm going to throw my drink in her face.'

I thought, 'Oh *no*!' The place was crawling with papparazzi and I could just see me with a drink tipped over me and headlines like 'Nasty Nina Gets Hers'. And I wasn't doing anything mischievous at all. She did a lot of storming out, as if she had a piece of elastic tied to her ankle. 'I'm going now, I said I'm going.' Then, 'If you don't come with me now, you're not getting into the hotel room.'

Silly bitch! He stayed with me instead. That was the beginning of more than just a fling, more of a serious relationship. He was much older than nineteen, though still a definite toyboy in relation to me.

To meet people like that you have to go out. Nobody ever actually beats your door down with an axe to get to meet you. So unless you fancy a Jehovah's Witness every six months, you have to venture out. Because I love to bop and I love to do it best with beautiful young men, I always go somewhere you can dance. While I'm aware of the age difference between me and men in their twenties, I don't think anything of it. I just know that I fancy them whereas I don't fancy older men at all.

Men are a different breed, but it takes women forever to realise it. I'm sure there are women in their sixties who still think men are like women except for the dangly bits. But it's *not* the dangly bits that are different, it's the head that's the most different part, and that's what causes most of the problems women have with men. Men might as well be elephants or dinosaurs as human beings, they are definitely not the same species as women.

Somebody once asked me what would the difference be

between men and women in twenty years' time. Would there be more equality? Would women have more independence? I think so, to a certain extent – but in the sixty or so years since women became emancipated, look how little has changed. Look how few women MPs there are, for instance. Not that one gives a damn about politicians. If you're going to lead a boring life, you might as well be a man. (I don't count Margaret Thatcher, she is not a woman but a token man. She is not the same breed as me, thank you very much.)

I think the trouble with men is caused by women. Not by you and me, the women I mean are their mothers. The balance between men and women will not swing in women's favour till women stop pandering to their sons. Women treat their sons differently from the way they treat their daughters. Is it because marriage is disappointing? Is it because the love they want to lavish on their husband gets channelled into their sons?

I think I've always done it wrong in relationships with men compared with women who always seem to get away with things: the sort of women who get away with whinge-ing that they can't cope, that they can't carry their suitcase. They burst into tears, they break their fingernails and it's the end of the world. But they survive – because there will always be men who fall all over themselves to cosset them. This form of female weakness feeds the male ego. His reaction is: this dear little thing needs me. 'Here, take a hundred pounds. Go and replace that fingernail'.

I suppose I spent too much of my life being Good Old Nina. To both men and women, I was the same. And I resented it – it's a terrible trap to fall into. It's as much of a trap as never having a man as a friend or being a woman who doesn't like other women. To be Good Old Nina to everybody means that's the way people treat you. It's fine if that's what you want but sometimes it gets very wearing being a Jolly Good Sport and having all these men telling you all their woes and troubles with other women – as if you weren't female or something. But if that happens to you, that's your own fault. It's a kind of barrier you put up, making yourself an honorary bloke. They like you and feel at ease with you because you're no threat – but I'd much rather *be* a threat.

Being Jolly Old Nina, carrying my own luggage and coping and having to pay my own bills does get up my nose from time to time. I get resentful and get the feeling I've done it wrong.

But I also know I could never get away with not coping, now. Because although I muddle through and muck along, I'll always cope. I can always be relied on. It's hard to believe men fall for the Little Woman trick, it staggers me that it works. I can only think it's because men are so stupid. They like to be able to pat women on the head or on the bum or preferably both. Patronising women makes men feel bigger or better. It makes some of the smaller-brained ones feel ten feet tall.

There is a TV programme controller I know of, who has the ultimate say on all sorts of light entertainment programmes and he is one of the most sexist pigs you could ever encounter. He talks about sex constantly. (I think men who talk about it like that obviously don't do it – or don't do it well enough.) He actually said to a female producer, 'You're wearing a new bra today aren't you? You look much perter, much perkier.' He said to another poor girl as he grabbed her by the hips, 'Are these your love-handles? Is this what your old man hangs on to?' Now there's an example of A Horrible Man. Sadly, there are lots of them about.

It's been fascinating to see the response I've had, as a TV critic, from men I've criticised. Any uncomplimentary remarks I've made have always produced a worse response from men than from women. I think it's because women mostly have a better sense of humour about themselves than men do, the male ego is so much more fragile.

People like Max Bygraves, Jimmy Tarbuck and even

Alan Coren don't like funny women or women who might be amusing: strong women terrify them. I'm sure that if they had confidence in themselves and their sexuality, they wouldn't worry about such women.

Young men are far more easy-going. You don't have to worry so much about stroking their egos as keeping up with their music, what band is current and what's not – and if you're pathetic about loud music, forget it. There's no way you can cope if you don't like multi-decibel sound.

On the other hand, it depends how long the relationship is going to last. If it's six hours, who cares what music they like? If it's going to be twelve hours, you better have a bit of conversation. If they're foreign and can't speak much English, that's probably all to the good. You don't have to put up with boring chat about football teams.

Everybody, whatever their age, is fascinated by sex. The mystique of bonking is that everyone wants to know what everyone else is doing and with whom. That's what gossip is about. It's the old Monty Python joke, the nudge-nudge, wink-wink sketch which ends up with Eric Idle saying, 'Did you do it? What was it like?' We're no further forward than that – that's what the whole tabloid press is about.

With bonking, nobody ever knows whether they're doing it right. There are times when you think perhaps everyone in the world knows the secret of doing it properly and you don't. The advantage of being older is that you've had more experience. A man I know in his early thirties said to me that one of the pleasures in going out with young girls is that they're so easy to impress. You just know so much more than them that they think you're terrific. When it comes to sex, you're bound to know what you're doing because you've done it more often. (Mind you, there are nineteen- and twenty-year-old boys who know exactly what they're doing. I sometimes think

28

they have at least as much experience as the average forty-year-old.)

I suppose that, without being a complete slut, the more different people you do it with, the more you learn. I also think that meeting men who really like women, not just to screw, makes all the difference.

Age makes you more confident about your body and yourself, not one hundred per cent confident, but considerably more certain about the mornings after.

A famous television actress once told me she woke up in a strange bed one morning with a huge hangover. As she looked across the room, directly in her line of vision was a pair of very small trainers. She couldn't remember anything of the night before and all she could think was, 'Oh God, I've fucked a dwarf.' She was terrified to turn round and see who was beside her. When she did, he was standard size: the trainers belonged to his nephew who was staying with him.

That's one of the reasons why I've always tried to go back to my own place with a new man. With somebody strange, going to their unknown habitat is too risky. At least in your own home you know where everything is. And you're not the one having to scuttle round looking for a dressing gown. (I don't leap up and rush round making cups of coffee next morning, either. If they want coffee, I point them towards the kitchen.)

Contrary to what most women think, men are far more romantic than women. Women are more practical. If a woman fancies a man she wants to get straight on with it. She may pretend to play games but when it comes down to it, if she's decided to Do It she'll want to do it *now*. On the other hand, if she's decided she's *not* going to Do It, she's not. *But mostly she is.* Men don't realise it and most women will never admit it, but that's how it is.

And after all, bonking is a pretty good way of burning up calories and getting the metabolism going. If you have a celibate period, everything shuts down, and you just don't feel as healthy or alive. I think sex is very fundamental to your well-being, it makes you feel good about yourself. A bonk a day keeps the fat away.

You don't have to be that fit, but you've only got to see some couples waddling round to wonder how they ever Do It. Perhaps they don't? Or maybe they do it very fast and with difficulty. Sometimes in an exercise class I look at a married woman and think, Her husband must have a really boring time. I always like to see a man dance. If he can't follow you on the dance floor he'll never do what you want in bed. You don't have to be the world's greatest athlete but if you can't bend or move, what kind of pleasure can it be?

All this is not to say that if you can't get laid you might as well be laid out. But almost. I suppose I am a bit of a lay preacher: I don't think everyone should have to battle through years of inhibition and prejudice and guilt before they can enjoy their sex life. Although it does depend on your upbringing; my mother was very down-to-earth and scientific about things sexual but the atmosphere in Scotland was not encouraging. Somehow it always seemed too freezing cold to Do It.

A lot of my early problems with men were caused by inability to cope. For a start, I could never believe that anybody really fancied me. And if you can't believe anyone fancies you, nobody will. It's the vibes you give out. If you're convinced you're not attractive, however much you spend on eye cream or however carefully you dress, if you don't feel sexually desirable inside yourself, you're not going to attract anyone. It's like dieting, you can't ever be thin unless you can picture yourself slimmer. You have to know what to aim for.

When I was overweight I wouldn't look at myself in the mirror without my clothes on because I hated the sight of myself. Therefore I wouldn't look in the mirror and see myself thin. And because I felt so clumsy or so unattractive physically, I couldn't imagine myself doing anything. If you don't have the confidence to run down the street or jump up and down, there's no way you're going to imagine yourself hanging off a chandelier.

Things have changed since then. I celebrated Christmas Day at 3 a.m. up a coconut tree in Bali with a Frenchman. And New Year's Day at 5 a.m. in a swimming pool with an Italian. So far there's never been a chandelier around when I've felt like a swing, but who knows? I can certainly hear the crystal tinkling.

What a load of bankers

Money certainly does make the world go round for me. It can buy enough champagne to make the world go round, and round and round. . . .

Although I'm passionate about pink, I seem to have spent most of my life in the red. Other people have a bank balance, but my approach to money is too unhinged for me to have any kind of balance.

Generations of bank managers have tried to explain it to me. Countless times I've sat opposite them while they tried to tell me how to do cheque stubs and I've just sat there nodding like a dog in the back window of a Cortina. I'd just say yes, take another cheque book and ignore the stubs again.

As a result of this particular failing, I now have to operate without a cheque book and without plastic – which sometimes leads to some interesting exchanges. On holiday in the Caribbean I met a man who gazed deep into my eyes and asked, what I did and when I told him I was a journalist he said, 'I've never met a journalist.'

I asked what he did. 'I'm a plastic surgeon.'

I replied, 'The only plastic surgeon I've ever met is my bank manager. He removed all my plastic with one slice.'

My credit finally ran out with a rush in South America where I was on a tour with Queen in 1981. We'd been drunk for days and were in Argentina after the last concert when Freddie Mercury took us all out to dinner. At about three in the morning we were all completely smashed when we descended on the hotel coffee shop and drank Bloody Marys till people started arriving for breakfast. When it got round to lunch and we were still drinking Bloody Marys we thought it was time to stop. But not for long. We then had to catch a plane to Rio and the only way to keep awake on the plane was to keep on drinking. On arrival in Rio we fell off the plane to find it was carnival time: everyone was samba-ing in two spangles and a whisp.

The story gets worse: three of us decided to lash out $100 each and go to the hotel carnival ball where one of the guys immediately ordered two bottles of champagne which we drank very fast. Then it was my turn to order. Paying with my American Express card, by that stage I was so out of control I was signing my name half on the form and half on the tablecloth. The local currency had trillions of noughts on the end and I had no idea what I was spending. Until I got home and discovered I'd paid £346 for two bottles of champagne.

I thought it was worth every penny but my bank manager didn't. He decided it was time to cut up my credit cards and take away my cheque book. Ouch.

My trouble is that I have the concentration of a mosquito. I can't listen to anyone talking about boring things (like money) for longer than three seconds. So whenever my bank manager told me I didn't have enough for a lettuce and tomato sandwich, let alone a shower of champagne, my mind was always wandering somewhere else – like in the direction of the next bottle of fizzy. It simply never occurred to me that I couldn't pay for the ice in my drinks, never mind the drinks.

I also have an aversion to brown envelopes which didn't help my case in clashes with the bank. Brown is such a depressing colour. I'm sure the only kind of person who would willingly open a brown envelope is the one who sends off for porn packages. Perhaps my bank realised that any message from them would read like an obscenity to me.

For a long time when all these brown letters from the bank plopped on to my doormat I didn't open them, I just carried them around with me in a plastic bag. In the end the bank pulled the plug on me and announced the end of our relationship. I had to hand back all the money I'd borrowed for home improvements, even though I had actually spent it on the home improvements. It didn't make a lot of sense to me: I could hardly de-fit my fitted kitchen and send it off in bits to the bank. And if I'd had the money to give back, I wouldn't have needed to borrow it in the first place. Maths was never my strong point but I could just work out that a stretch of work-tops plus a stack of shelves, a stove and fridge did not add up to money in the bank or anywhere else. I had to re-mortgage my flat to pay back the loan – and take my business elsewhere.

Being expelled by the bank was worse than, I imagine, being expelled from school. At least you've got the foolishness of youth to blame for the latter. There is not a lot of sympathy around for big girls whose cheques bounce. Cheques, I said.

No other bank would take me. It seemed my old bank was going before me, ringing a bell like those people who warn about lepers. When I tried to put my salary cheque into a bank, it was as if the door was barred by an angel with a flaming sword. The word had got around.

But I got my own back. Not being a particularly vengeful person, I am nevertheless elephantine in my unforgetfulness. I always trust that things come full circle – and they usually do. I can wait, though. Believe me, I can wait. And I waited till I got my revenge on my old bank.

When it came to the final parting they came up with one last sum of £347.75 in interest which I had to pay. As I had handed over £1,000 only the month before, I was less than penniless. As I said to my solicitor, 'Even supposing I *could* write a cheque, I wouldn't have to take

34

it to the bank, it would bounce there all by itself.'

That was when revenge came to mind. I asked my solicitor if what I had in mind was legal – and it was. So I took a taxi to another bank and collected a hundred pounds in twenty-pence pieces, a hundred pounds in ten-pence pieces, a hundred pounds in fives, forty-seven pounds in twos and seventy-five pence in ones.

It was so heavy that the taxi-driver had to help me carry it into the taxi, all packed into five bright red sacks. When I told him what I was going to do, he said, 'I'd hate to get on the wrong side of you, darlin'.' But after I told him why I was doing it, he was with me all the way. When we pulled up outside my old bank, he got in the back and helped me unwrap the coins and mix them all up. It was like kids making mud-pies. By the time I stormed through the bank doors I could practically hear the 'Ride of the Valkyries' playing.

I had an appointment with a woman with a long pointy nose through which she spoke and down which she looked. 'Miss Myskow, how can I help you?' she asked in a Miss Jean Brodie accent.

'I believe I owe you £347.75.'

'I'll just check that.'

'Don't worry, I've checked it. Can you just wait a moment?' I went outside and called, 'Oi, Bert, in 'ere.' My taxi driver carried in three sacks while I staggered under two.

The expression on Miss Brodie's face will stay with me until my dying day. Her jaw dropped and she went absolutely white and clutched her face. 'Oh, Miss Myskow,' she said, 'I didn't think we'd be getting it like this.'

'That's exactly why you *are* getting it like this,' I said.

She was still clutching her pallid cheeks as she asked, 'What kind of coinage is it?'

'Every coinage possible. Have fun counting it! Have a nice day!' I trilled. Then we stormed out of the bank and drove off down Piccadilly like Bonnie and Clyde, yelling out of the window.

When he dropped me back in Fleet Street he said, 'They're never gonna believe me when I tell 'em about this back at base. What am I going to do with the rest of my day? It'll be all downhill from here.'

I knew exactly how he felt.

What I learned from the whole experience was that banks are run by very simple people whose brains work along very straight lines. That's why they become bankers – because they have no imagination or creativity. They think it's heaven to write a boring letter and to get a boring letter back. Or better still, a boring phone call. They're not stupid, they just have a certain way of operating.

The secret in making your bank your best friend is to stay in touch. As long as they know what's going on, they can do deals with you. You tell them you want a new car and they tell you you can't have one (unless it costs less than £15.42 and you can pay it back in luncheon vouchers over the next two minutes).

It's a game, but I can't play it. I'd rather play strip poker or even postman's knock. And I'd much rather keep my money under the mattress – only with my spending habits I couldn't always be sure there was a mattress at home to put the money under. Or even a home for the missing mattress.

What has now sorted me out is an accountant, one of a race of men I used to be rude about. I have now totally changed my mind about them. Mine is called Alan and I am a much better-balanced woman because of him. I am even in the black occasionally – specially the little black by Gaultier or Galliano, Armani or Alaia. He opens all my envelopes and even though I have to ask him before I can buy so much as a new toothbrush, I don't mind. He's on the case. And he has a sense of humour. He has to!

Being mature about money is knowing you're a child with it. You own up and say, 'I hate all this, I don't like doing it,' – and let someone else do it for you. There's no point in cheating someone who's on your side (though I still find myself sliding round him from time to time).

My philosophy with money and everything else is: too much is not enough. I *love* spending money and luckily I'm actually quite good at making it. It's just that I'm better at spending it. And I definitely don't see the point in saving it.

They say you should save up for your old age. Well this *IS* my old age and I've got to spend it. Better to splash out now on *getting* the wrinkles and the eyebags than later on having them fixed up. When you're too old for anyone to fancy you, why bother?

Somehow I've always managed to pay my own way: I own my own flat, I buy my own cars, my own clothes, my own jewellery, I pay for my own holidays, my food, my drinks, my rates, my gas bill – and my toyboys.

I've always simply spent more than I've earned. I've always spent to the limit, and as far as I could push it and get away with it until somebody stopped me. And then I've earned enough to pay it back. (I should add that I've never borrowed from people, only banks.) I used to get cross when friends with rich husbands got critical of the scrapes I found myself in. I wanted to ask them, 'Okay, when did you buy your last holiday or your own car? Do you pay for the roof over your own head?'

I'm very twitchy about money in some areas. I don't like people paying for things for me. With men, I've always paid half and half. If I go on holiday with someone, I pay my own way. I like to be independent and I don't like to feel bought. I can't stand the idea of a guy buying me dinner then feeling he has bought the right to grope me. That's a horrible concept. I like to feed myself and feel free.

The first money I ever earned was from D.C. Thomson's in Dundee in October 1966, a week's salary in a little brown envelope which jingled: it was seven pounds and ten shillings. Even in 1966 it was godawful money. So I thought, 'I'm going to spend it on something I don't need. Not something like scent or make-up, but something that I'll always try to keep to remind me how ridiculous money is.' So I bought a pair of shocking pink stockings which cost about a pound. I still have them to remind me how hard I worked for rubbish money. I may get them framed one day.

But even when the amount has been pitiful, I have always been really grateful to be paid for anything I did. However, there are things I'm learning not to do, no matter how much is offered.

I should have known better, for instance, than to agree to co-compere a Mr Wet Y-fronts competition in a London suburban club. When my agent first told me about it, I said no. Then he said: 'Don't say no till you've heard it all. It's in Ealing.' I said no. He repeated. 'Mr Wet Y-fronts.' I said no. 'Only forty-five minutes.' No. 'It's a thousand pounds.' Er, yeah, okay. . . .

It was way past my bedtime (it took place at one in the morning) and it was in Ealing. I don't mind dancing till dawn in the West End, but Ealing! It's so boring I don't know how anyone even wakes up there.

Alarm bells rang in my head when I saw a photographer and a fairly dodgy-looking agent awaiting my arrival. It was all so demeaning: I realised I would rather die than let anyone know I'd been there. It was like finding out too late that you're top-of-the-bill down at your local's amateur strip night. Only this was professional and I had to deliver.

I was supposed to interview the guys as they came on and then make saucy comments about them. But the words choked in my throat – I thought they were just so revolting. Think about it: even Mel Gibson or Tom Cruise would lose some of their charm if they came at you in wet Y-fronts. For godssake, dry Y-fronts are bad enough. The only thing you can say about Y-fronts is 'Y-wear-'em?' The only thing you could do was turn it into a joke. So when one said he was a carpenter, I asked if it was because he was wooden from the neck up. The girls in the audience all agreed with me and started cheering.

I refused to pose for the photographer afterwards and my fellow compere refused to speak to me. It was not my finest hour and I am happy that I was never invited back.

That experience made up my mind. However much I needed a quick thousand bucks, to go to Turkey or Thailand or Timbuktu – or to buy a couple of over-priced bottles of champagne at a time of night when I could barely pronounce it – if I had to compromise myself by doing something I hated, forget it.

And that includes judging talent, a skill I am known for but which I decided to drop after a disastrous experience with an Australian television producer. He hired me for five shows then sat and watched while we taped shows one and two. He then spent the last three shows threatening death and destruction if I didn't tone down my act and be more positive about the contestants. By positive he meant flattering.

Hell, they must have known what I was like before they hired me. It has always been my policy to tell the truth, to say what everyone at home on the sofa is thinking. That way, I believe, you spare not only the public but the performer any more embarrassment than is necessary. You're doing everyone a favour. Our hot-shot producer should have known that you don't hire a tap dancer if you want someone to play the piano.

I was due to record five more shows in the same series but I pulled out. Some people would say, I suppose, that that was being stupid about money. A more money-smart person than I might have thought that for £1,500 for one day's work they could force themselves to say anything the producer wanted.

I have been known to describe myself as an ageing amateur bimbo and apprentice bag lady – bag lady because I'm ludicrous with money and feckless. If I don't end up pushing my belongings in a pram around the streets one day it will be a minor miracle.

My friends are always telling me I can come and live in their spare rooms when things go wrong. One couple are saving the Wendy house in their garden for when I fall on harder times. They say they'll just move the mower out and I can move in.

Of course, there is always half a chance I'll achieve the opposite of trampdom and make big, big money (we can all dream). And I would *not* be one of those people who claim they would remain unchanged by riches. I'd still make sure I spent more than I earned. But I'd live in a bigger Chateau Squalor than I do now. I'd do everything *bigger*.

I go through phases when I have no money at all – like when the bank threw me out. I have found myself with only ten pounds to see me through the weekend and I couldn't do anything with it. What's a tenner? It's a bottle of supermarket champagne and a packet of crisps; a rented video, a Big Mac and four tins of XXXX; three Bloody Marys and a peanut – whatever way you look at it, it's only a good time for a very few moments.

I don't like dealing only in cash as I do now because there's no safety net there. You can't do what everyone else does when the purse runs dry: produce the plastic or sprint to the hole-in-the-wall. But I know if I had plastic and a cheque book, I would just spend and spend.

There's something magic about writing cheques. But now I only do it once a month and under strict supervision. When I turn up at Alan's, they practically bring in the cheque book on a silver salver with the cheques filled out for me to sign – which I do in pink ink and with a flourish. I don't think of plastic as money, but cheques certainly have the taste of the real thing.

A friend of mine was diagnosed as a diabetic and when they asked him how much he drank they gasped and said, 'That much!' He told me, 'I suppose I'll really have to change my habits. But I only really feel happy after the third pint like you only feel happy after the third cheque.'

It's true. It almost feels like getting drunk. You write one and you feel better, you write another and feel great and you just start going for it. It was such pure happiness. . . .

I long to use those hole-in-the-wall machines again, as well. When friends say they have to get some money from one, I ask if I can go along and watch. It's magic watching the fresh notes coming out.

I had one of those cards once. You know how they give you a number and ask you to memorise it and throw the bit of paper away? They tell you an easy way to learn it is to replace the numbers with letters, A for one, B for two and so on. No prizes for guessing what four-letter word mine spelled: that's why I minded so much when I had to give it back!

I suppose I'm very lucky in that I've often been around people who had a lot of money. So I've vicariously lived a rich existence from time to time. For an evening, or a day or even a weekend. At the risk of sounding like some hanger-on with palm permanently outstretched, there is nothing quite like the ride in the Bentley in the middle of the night with the sound system going and arriving at Brown's for more champagne.

Elton John is like that. I've known him since about 1969, just after he changed his name from Reg. I was the fashion editor of *Jackie* magazine in Dundee at the time and we were introduced by a London fashion contact who said, 'Come and meet this new singer-songwriter.'

We went to a caff in the Tottenham Court Road and got on like a house on fire, we had the same daft sense of humour. When I went back to Scotland he wrote to say let's keep in touch. Then he sent me the demo tape of 'Your Song' – my heart still turns over every time I hear it.

Shortly afterwards, I made (one of) the biggest mistake(s) of my whole life. I arranged to have lunch with Elton on one of my visits to London and when we sat down we realised we were both very depressed: I hated Scotland and I hated fashion, which was full of boring old cows panicking all the time; Elton had just recorded his first album, 'Empty Sky', and was worrying that he couldn't write any more because he had parted company with his lyricist, Bernie Taupin

He asked me whether I had ever written lyrics. I hadn't. Then he said, 'When you go back to Scotland, write me some lyrics and send them to me.'

If I had written just *one* that worked, banks would by now have been fighting to keep my custom.

Now I have to settle for living small segments of the luxury life at the expense of very generous friends. When Elton won his famous libel case against the *Sun*, there was a grand sit-down dinner to celebrate at his manager John Reid's place. There we were, thirty of us, sitting in a room with a Rembrandt on the wall. And John had bought fantastic presents for everybody, a lovely pair of earrings for me and a book called *The World's Most Wicked Women* (which he said I should be in).

Dinner had finished at 1 a.m. and I had to be home because I was having fifty people to a champagne tea party next afternoon. But someone said, 'Let's go to Brown's.' So we roared through the night to the club where there was vintage pink champagne and we ordered a bowl of caviar. A bowl? A week's wages would buy enough to fit on a cornflake but we were eating it from a thing like a fruit bowl, almost digging our bare hands in.

Now that's what money can buy. But I haven't got that sort of money and if I never make that sort of money, at least I've tasted what it can provide.

Perhaps that's very shallow. But I've been very lucky. I've been through times, when I was about seventeen, when I had one skirt and one jumper. We didn't have any money and I didn't like that. I didn't feel sorry for myself – but I thought I'd rather have money than not.

Love of it may be the root of all evil. All I can say is, it can be the start of some wonderfully evil moments. . . .

A bread-basket case

Some of the best times I've ever had are when I go bread-basketing, as it's become known.

It started on the Caribbean island of Montserrat, where I was sent to interview a band called The Tourists, who later made it very big as The Eurythmics. They were out there recording at George Martin's Air Studios and on the last night, when the album was finished, it was traditional to celebrate with a goat barbecue.

We all roared down to the beach where there was a goat rotating on a spit. I knew I was up for trouble. They had forgotten to bring a corkscrew so, for starters, I was pulling my top trick of getting a cork out without an opener: you wrap the bottom in a towel and tap it gently against a wall. Either the cork comes out or the bottle shatters. This time, luckily it worked. The party was on its way.

There was a steel band and it was really good fun, a great night. Don't remember much about it except that we all had a good time. However, next morning I woke feeling like I'd just fallen down a mineshaft. Dreadful. The only thing to do was to go for a swim: either I'd drown, which would get rid of some of my problems, or I'd feel better.

As I staggered back from the beach, not sure if I felt better or whether I'd have preferred drowning, I ran into the representative from Air Studios in New York, one of those women who is two inches wide, has minuscule hips and wears nothing but beige. My favourite sort of woman. She said, 'Why don't you join us for lunch?' It was the last thing I felt like. But I went, and once I'd had a Bloody Mary, things started to brighten up.

Everyone was saying what a good party it had been and suddenly the woman-in-beige said to me, 'My, but you were funny last night.' Everyone laughed, but she went on, 'No, but really, you were so funny.' I said I was glad I had provided some entertainment but, actually, what were they talking about?

'You don't remember?'

'No, I don't remember.'

'You don't remember the steel band?'

'Of course I remember the steel band.'

'You don't remember falling into and knocking over the entire front row of the steel band?'

I thought, oh God, that's what that bruise is.

Everyone laughed again, then there was a long silence. Then she looked at me and said, 'That wasn't the funniest part.'

'Oh no?'

'The funniest part was, you were wearing a bread basket on your head at the time.'

Thank you very much, lady.

That's how it became known as bread-basketing. When my friends ring up after a night out and I've got a hangover, they always ask, 'Was it a bread-basket?' and I have to say, 'No, half a bread-basket', or, 'Nearly a bread-basket'.

I always say I've done some wonderful things, drunk, in my time – and I wish I could remember most of their names.

I don't know really how I still survive. There was a time in Turkey when I went for a cruise on a boat with twelve passengers and three crew. We anchored in a beautiful bay to have dinner in a village which was up the hillside.

It was somebody's birthday and there was lots of drinking and smashing of glasses.

God knows what time we all rolled down the mountainside on our way back but when we got to the beach we remembered that the dinghy which was going to take us back to the boat only took six people. So the locals said, don't make two trips, we'll take the rest in our motor boats.

We then had a race around the bay in the dark in the two boats and I came to, so to speak, when I realised I was standing with one foot on one boat, and one foot on the other.

I blame this on the Polish spirit and I don't mean just the vodka. It's a nation that has cavalry-charged tanks. Pig-headed and reckless, you could say we Poles are.

I used to drink quite a lot of vodka but now I cannot refuse champagne. Mind you, I don't know anyone who, when asked, 'Will you have some champagne?' will reply, 'No thank you, not for me.' At least, I suppose there are such people but I don't want to know them.

Most people associate champagne with success but I just associate it with excess. I drink it till either the bottle's gone flat or I have. Once you start, I don't see the point in stopping till you've actually drained the magnum.

The trouble with champagne, though, is it makes me lose things. I've lost my balance with it. I've lost my earrings, and I once lost a millionaire.

He was a film and television producer and a friend had set me up with him. He had been married three times and had numerous affairs and was totally not my type. He was older than me and the sort of chap who, if you walked through a door you had opened yourself, would take great offence. 'Oh, *you're* playing the chap tonight', he'd say. A very sweet man, totally nice, do anything for you but . . .

One night we went to a very grand ball at the Dorchester, just after the second hearing of the court case in which I was sued by the actress Charlotte Cornwell. I had hardly eaten for two weeks, I had been very stressed and nervous but by then I felt a sense of relief. Dressed up in my ball gown I felt life was possible again. I was wearing this lovely shocking pink silk Roland Klein number with a fichu neckline and a big skirt – which became known thereafter as the Behaving Badly Frock. So I had the frock, somewhere to wear it, someone to go with. I felt wonderful.

As soon as we got there, he bought two vodkas and they were followed by lashings of champagne. We had a great time, lovely table we were at, lovely people. We were dancing and drinking, drinking and dancing. It was marvellous.

Then I found myself dancing with someone not from our table and time had ceased to have meaning. When I got back to our table, the woman who had invited me said, 'He's gone.'

'What do you mean, he's gone?'

'He's left, he just walked out.'

At that point I was too far gone to care but in the morning, when I thought about it, I felt awful. For this man, whose manners were impeccable, to walk out he must have been really upset and very cross.

Then I realized he would have to contact me because he had my big brooch which had fallen off and he'd put it in his pocket to look after it.

I rang a few friends, my hangover was easing but I felt deeply depressed. I kept asking myself, 'Why do you feel so bad? Is it because you drank too much or are you cross because this man walked out?'

But as I went to go out to lunch I found a package which had been pushed through my door. In it was my brooch and a note which read, 'Dear Nina, I waited for you for nearly an hour. Then I left. Signed . . .'

That was it. I knew the drawbridge was up. I felt even more depressed.

That night I got in the bath, put on a face pack and had a large glass of wine. I never drink alone but I felt so down, I thought what the hell. And I sat in the bath drinking the glass of wine out of the side of my mouth so as not to disturb the face pack. Then the phone rang and I leaped out, roared into the living room and said, still out of the corner of my mouth (it was an expensive face-pack, I didn't want to waste it), 'Whossat?'

'Martin', said a man's voice.

'Who?'

'Do you remember *anything* from last night?'

I had to say no, he would have to start filling me in on details.

'Where shall I start?'

'Well you could start with your name', I suggested.

'I can see why you've forgotten it. It's a very complicated name – Smith.'

I remembered nothing.

He said I had agreed to go out with him and all I could say in astonishment was, 'Did I?'

'How do you think I got your number?' he asked. I had to admit that was a good point.

So we arranged to go out and I said, 'I'd better give you the address.'

'I've got it', he said. 'And I know how to get there and to ring the middle bell.'

There was no getting out of that one.

I never heard from my millionaire friend again and from then onwards whenever I wore my big pink frock I behaved badly in it.

I put it on for the British Association of Film and Television Awards, which I was supposed to attend with Elton John's manager, John Reid. But in the end he sent the Bentley and the tickets and I went on my own. Dates with Reid are best written in your diary in pencil. (Or invisible ink.)

You have to get there very early, about 5.30 p.m., and

have drinks and dinner before it starts. Then you drink during it and after it. So you're drinking for *hours*. No wonder Julie Walters nearly fell over that year when she went to get her award. I'm amazed more people don't. You can tell the really arrogant ones who think they've won prizes – they're the ones who've remained sober.

I was just up for fun, really. But that was before Janet Street Porter produced some pink champagne, always my downfall. I was idly chatting away to some TV people including a little chap from one of the soaps who was very persistently trying to move in on me. I kept trying to brush him aside but, what with one thing and another, I found myself in a taxi with him, heading for his hotel.

As we were going up in the lift to his suite, I kept thinking to myself, 'What am I doing?' I asked him how old he was and he replied, 'Nineteen'.

I said, '*Nobody's* nineteen. When were you born?' And he told me. He'd got it right, he really *was* nineteen.

But there we were and he was actually terrific. (And if you could have seen me next morning, scuttling across the foyer of the hotel in the Behaving Badly Frock trying to pretend I was dressed normally . . . well, fortunately not many people did.)

The BBF had another outing to a very grand ball, at which you had to wear nineteenth-century dress or evening dress, in the grounds of Chiswick House in aid of the Royal Academy. As a result of cavorting in the shrubbery at one stage that night, the Behaving Badly Frock is now reduced to ballerina-length.

That ball was on one of those nights, so beautiful in the garden, that you wanted it to go on forever. I never want to go home – that's my trouble. But at two o'clock they served breakfast, with apologies that they only had a licence to go on till three.

When a woman explained this to us, of course I was the one who had to get all stroppy and say, 'Who says so? Who the hell are you?' And, inevitably, she turned out to be Lady Someone-or-other who was on the committee.

Awful. I didn't even know her and there I was, slagging her off while I rummaged in the hair-piece I was wearing and which was about to fall off. I don't like to remember that moment at all.

It's the champagne that does it. I have practised saying to people who ask if I'd like another drink, 'No thank you, I already have one.' I say it over and over again. But when the time comes, I actually quite like to see the drinks lined up.

There are horror stories about women drinking but I don't identify with them at all. I suppose it's because I don't do it all that often. I don't drink on a consistent, steady basis. It's just that when I do, I get bread-basketed and don't seem to have any control.

Hopefully, friends forgive me my behaviour but I'm not quite sure about other people. I feel guilty, to a certain extent, if I've done something really ghastly, but it doesn't stop me from doing the same all over again.

I once interviewed Julie Walters when *Educating Rita* came out and afterwards I drove her into the West End where we decided, on the spur of the moment, to have lunch. It was a quarter to three when we stepped into the bar of the Coconut Grove and asked for two silly drinks: pina coladas made pink.

The waiter looked at us and said, 'I feel obliged to tell you that these drinks have to be off the table by three.'

'In that case,' I said, 'we'll have another four.'

So we had three each in fifteen minutes – and I'm amazed we weren't arrested afterwards for going shoplifting or something equally appalling. I don't even remember how I got home.

I learned to drink young. Where I was brought up in South Africa, in Pietermaritzburg, there were what we called The Local Boys. They were Polish and the Allies had dispersed them throughout the colonies because they couldn't get back to Poland. There were about twenty of them, adolescent guys, in our town. My father and others

49

made sure these kids were okay and working and had money and they used to organise a big Polish Christmas Eve for them because that's when the Poles celebrate Christmas, not on Christmas Day. So I was lucky, I had two goes at it.

The feast was tremendous, twelve courses, between each of which was served a little glass of neat vodka. When I was about eight I was sitting down the opposite end of the table from my mother and I managed to get to the fifth course and the fifth glass of vodka, whoosh, straight down the throat, before she caught me. I think that's where I got my head for vodka.

There have been great gaps in my life where I haven't drunk at all. I didn't drink in Scotland, though I can't think why – I hated the place so much.

I never had a hangover till I was well over thirty. I used to wonder what it was like, when I saw films with people wandering round clutching their heads. I couldn't understand. I used to wonder what this over-dramatic nonsense was and what was *wrong* with these people.

And then I had a hangover. I remember my first one, I was wiped out. It lasted all day. It must be old age that makes the after-effects so much worse. And there's nothing that helps. I get to the stage where the only thing I can cope with is nursery food, like rice pudding or ice cream: solid carbohydrate stuff. When I fancy rice pudding, I know that hangover's a bad one.

There is no cure. I've tried having Beecham's Resolve before I go to sleep and as soon as I wake up. But it doesn't help. You just have to live through it somehow. There's no way round it, the only great comfort to be found is when everybody else feels as bad as you.

The best thing to do is stay in bed, pull the duvet over your head, take the phone off the hook and ask yourself why you did it? This is when you vow not to do it again. But you forget. And then the next time you're drinking at five o'clock in the morning, having a really good time, you can't imagine that you'll feel ill, ever, because you feel so good *then*.

I think it's going to bed that does it. Cut out sleeping – that's the answer.

As far as drink goes, I don't know much about quality. There are all these connoisseurs who know about different cognacs and what sort of grape does what and what a claret is. I don't know what a claret is. And probably couldn't tell the difference between red and white blindfolded.

When I gave up drinking and driving people said, 'Just have one glass of wine', I had to ask what was the point of one glass of wine? Why not have one bottle?

That was when I realised that whatever reasons other people drink for, or what they say they drink for, I drink to get drunk. Not necessarily falling-over drunk, though that quite often happens, but definitely to feel mellow. I drink because I like the effect it has on me – and I don't know why nobody else seems to admit this.

I've got no time for the people who drink non-alcoholic wines. Why torture yourself? These little vintages taste disgusting and they don't do you any harm. They may do you good but who wants that? If I want to drink something that does me good, I'll drink Horlicks or Lucozade.

I can't understand people who don't appreciate that wonderful moment when you start to feel slightly happy and life feels good. Then there's the actual falling-off-the-bar-stool stage when you don't care. And there's losing the earrings and throwing your shoes at people. That sort of getting drunk is lovely.

And then you get to the smoking stage: I only smoke when I'm drunk and only special long thin pink cigarettes. I don't really smoke them, just wave them about a lot. When people see the pink cigarettes come out, they know it's time to run for cover.

I was at a ball for the Starlight Charity at Grosvenor House one memorable night in the Behaving Badly Frock when the champagne flowed and the cigarettes wafted – a night just right for a bread-basket.

There were lots of rock 'n' roll and show business people there, like Paul Young and Spandau Ballet, and I was with a guy from A and M Records in a party of record company people. In the middle of the ball there was a charity auction hosted by Jeremy Beadle, helped by Jonathan Ross and Gary Davies who were fielding the bids.

They were auctioning things like a trip to Paris and George Michael's leather jacket, lots of sweaty rockers' items you would have paid £10,000 *not* to have. There was also a prize of five days' tuition at Brands Hatch, with the chance to take part in a race at the end of it – which the girl across the table from me started bidding for, at £11,000.

When Gary Davies relayed this back, Jeremy Beadle launched into a whole load of sexist rubbish about women drivers, 'What's a woman doing bidding for this?' he prattled.

The girl's face fell to the table and I thought, 'What sodding cheek.' I had a few glasses of champagne inside me and I waited till Gary scooted past again and demanded, 'Give me that microphone.'

He was like a startled rabbit caught in headlights, there was no escape.

'Mr Beadle', I began. He couldn't tell where it was coming from, this disembodied voice, so he just kept blathering on.

I was back at the table by now, so I stood up for him to see me. 'For God's sake, Nina, why don't you sit down? Don't we have to see enough of you on Saturdays?' Beadle boomed. Everyone laughed.

'Mr Beadle', I persisted. 'It occurs to me that if a woman is prepared to bid £11,000 for charity, what she doesn't need is a whole load of sexist crap from you.'

There was thunderous applause.

Being me, I was so pleased with myself I drank buckets and buckets of champagne after that.

Then there was a raffle. And I was the lucky winner of

ten albums and a bowler hat belonging to Suggs from Madness. And I had to go up to the stage to get my prize.

I was so out of it I can't remember who I received it from. But unfortunately I do remember, only too well, that after I collected my prize I fell off the stage.

Chateau Squalor

My flat is known as Chateau Squalor because I decided long ago that I wasn't going to waste time cleaning it. I don't do domestics. I feel guilty about this but I don't see why anybody should do them unless they want to.

I don't Hoover because I don't enjoy it. But I'm lucky enough to be able to pay somebody to do it for me: my answer to all domestic problems is Vera, who comes in once a week to try to rearrange the muck. She fights a losing battle but as long as she's happy about that, I'm happy about that.

I certainly don't Hoover in between times. If I've got people coming on Wednesday and she comes on Thursday I don't rush round cleaning up. And I never apologise. If anybody should point out the dust, I just tell them, 'Vera comes tomorrow. So – tough.'

I used to scuttle about trying to get my place straight. It's not that I'm not logical, not that I can't be organised. I just can't be bothered. I can do all those things if I put my mind to it – but my brain won't allow me to do it. As my friend Caroline says, seeing me at home is like watching a giant hamster rummaging. I shuffle about making little pointless tracks in the straw.

I'd rather do something more interesting: like lying in a bath, talking on the telephone, painting my toenails or reading the back of the oatflakes packet to see if I can lower my cholesterol level in just ten weeks.

I just don't notice mess. I've been called a room wrecker: walks into a room, destroys it. I just drop things and within seconds it's a mess. And things can just lie where they drop till they become part of the decor. I think it's because I'm Taurean, like my friend Mary. Perhaps all Taureans are sluts? She is a fabulous cook and wonderful homemaker, but her husband Joe says she can drop a pair of tennis shoes in the middle of the kitchen floor and just walk around them for a week, radar-guided, without even looking at them. She knows they're there but she doesn't pick them up.

I'm like that as well. Sometimes when people are coming I have a little panic and open the cupboard door in the hall and throw everything in, one on top of the other, then jam the door shut. It is all piled up on top of my Amstrad, a Christmas present from me to me which hasn't come out of its box for two years.

They say you can organise your whole life with a personal computer – but it practically takes your whole life to organise the computer. For a start it's on a computer trolley which it took me approximately five hours to construct in front of the television. Why should anyone have to construct furniture? Furniture makers make furniture, why should customers have to do it? I'm in the business of buying furniture, not making it. Yet when I bought this trolley which I saw standing up in one piece in Habitat, it turned up all in bits in a box. Why do they do this to people?

I got the diagram out and all the different screws, with A, B, C and D, showing the way they went. You had to push all these tubular bits together before you screwed them up and there were holes which you had to put different shaped screws into before slotting everything around.

After I'd constructed two-thirds of it, I dropped one of the screws into one of the tubes. By this stage it was like a big climbing frame and I had to get inside it to retrieve the screws. So there I was, on my living room floor, trapped inside a climbing frame. I thought, 'I *do* want to do something constructive about my life – *but this isn't it*!'

I did finish putting it together, the computer fitted on it – and it's been sitting in the hall cupboard ever since, with the rubbish of centuries piling up on top of it. This is positively the last brush I ever hope to have with DIY anything. So if you're going to join me as a member of SODS – Stamp Out Domestics – you must never ever buy self-assembly furniture.

As for carpets, I have the least useful colour a person like me could ever have: cream. I now know why people buy those nightmare-patterned carpets in orange, black and brown that look like something regurgitated by a waste-disposal unit: they don't show dirt. And everything you drop on them disappears into the pattern. Whoever designed those was not a colour-blind cretin as previously thought, but a genius.

I'm quite happy in Chateau Squalor, where I've lived since 1979, but for some reason it still feels temporary to me. I suppose it's because I'm always poised for flight somewhere. It certainly isn't designed for people to stay, at least not for more than twelve hours or so. And that's deliberate. I don't mind lending the sofa out occasionally but I draw the line at anyone staying for ages. I can't stand the idea of anyone under foot (no, not even Mel Gibson – I'd prefer him in a different position). You get very selfish when you live by yourself, very used to your own space or lack of it. You need to be able to know your boundaries. Besides, house guests make housework.

My one domestic act is cleaning the bath. I think this comes from having shared a flat with other girls where the one thing everyone does, however slovenly they are, is clean the bath. Because if you don't, everyone thinks you're dirty. But I can't claim to be very good at it because it never occurs to me to shop for Vim or Fairy Liquid or whatever you need to do the job. I always have to be reminded by Vera and a week's pile of dirty dishes.

I suppose I should get into gadgetry and mechanical

things and have a little dishwasher and a little washing machine. But I don't even know how to use a washing machine and I don't want you to tell me how. I'm very happy letting my local Dot Cotton do my laundry.

I don't believe in microwaves and don't know what to do with them, either. I go to people's places and they say, 'Just put it in the microwave, will you?' and I have to admit I don't know what they're talking about and I'd rather they didn't explain.

Some gadgets do appeal, though, specially big daft gadgets. I've got an electric peanut butter-making machine which I bought in Los Angeles the first time I went there, in 1973, on an Elton John bunfight. It was the Elton John Rock of the Westies (West of the Rockies, geddit?) tour where he took a planeload of family and friends over to the West Coast for a week. I'd never been to America before, it was such a big thrill. He put us up in a Holiday Inn in Westwood, in a little area near UCLA, one of the few places in L.A. you can actually walk around without being arrested.

I was walking round this department store on my first day, just seeing what was different and what it all cost and my eye fell on this amazing machine. All you do is put the peanuts in the top end, switch it on and peanut butter comes out the bottom end. What made me decide to buy it is the dial on the side that says, Smooth or Crunchy. Who could resist? But of course I don't use it. Its major drawback is that you need a transformer to use it in Britain – and I've never got round to buying one.

I've got a wok, too, which my brother gave me. He said, 'You've got to have one of these.' Well, I can think of things to do with it, none of them involving food. You could wear it as a hat or plant flowers in it or use it as a satellite dish. Now *there's* a permanent, twenty-four-hour use for it: all those unused woks lying senseless at the backs of cupboards could be got out and made to wok around the clock.

When I got my kitchen installed, instead of going to

the Kitchen Centre or one of the fitted kitchen companies and saying, 'Put your units in, do your stuff', I listened to a friend. She told me about another friend who was an architect whose mother designed kitchens and said, 'He can do it for you'. Why, oh why, didn't I get the guy's mum to do it? But I was so bedazzled by his architectural drawings and him being clever and everything, that I just said yes.

It cost me a fortune – and it could only have been designed by a man. There is no way you can be happy cooking in this kitchen. It's got great storage space, all hung from a sort of hi-tech scaffolding, but there is absolutely no working space. Bloody useless.

I do love cooking, but not sensible things. Cakes are my speciality. Not that I'm saying making cakes is artistic – I leave that to Jane Asher.

Now there's a woman who doesn't know how to enjoy herself. She obviously doesn't like cakes or she'd spend more time eating them and not making them into perfect little choo choo trains, chocolate houses and footballs. Yet she makes a fortune inventing these horrible cakes for people. I'm sure there must be housewives everywhere making the ghastly things, thinking if they bake a cake like that they'll end up looking like Jane Asher. Forget it! If you want ginger eyelashes, have them dyed.

No, the way I bake cakes, you start off with a whole lot of ingredients and you end up with something concrete. Or perhaps I could put that a better way. . . .

I've had one dinner party in the past year, an Italian dinner party because I'd had an affair with Fabio, an Italian whom I had to put back where I found him. So I thought, 'If you can't have an Italian, have an Italian dinner party'. I was determined I wasn't going to serve any pasta at all, that would be too corny. So I went to an incredible amount of trouble to avoid everyone's favourite diet downfall.

Well, it wasn't disastrous. It was just one of those nights I wished I'd never thought of. The two Italians I'd asked cancelled at six o'clock on the evening of the dinner so I had to scrabble round for more people. And at two hours' notice you couldn't be too fussy about nationality. So much for the Italian theme. The food was all right but I was so slow with it, by the time everyone started eating they were completely clobbered by the chianti. I might as well have served takeaway pizza – never mind the pizza, they'd have eaten the box. Maybe that's the secret of a good dinner party: lots of booze to start off with – and who notices the food?

You might as well not bother about the food too much, either. I mean, why slave over it for hours when you can get a complete dinner party from Marks and Spencer? I don't believe anyone cooks any more – or, therefore, needs to clean an oven. If only we could fuel ourselves intravenously that would put an end to washing up as well.

Chateau Squalor's finest hour was when Loyd Grossman came to film for 'Through the Keyhole', the guess-which-star-lives-here programme. What a test of endurance that is – much worse than a dinner party. You can't just hide things in cupboards.

In fact, when 'Through the Keyhole' rang up to book me, I thought they were asking me to be on the panel again so I just said yes. But when they told me the cameras were coming round in September I realised my terrible mistake. I can't let them come to my place, I thought, they can't possibly film in Chateau Squalor.

I was away for a week just before filming was due to start and if it hadn't been for my amazing friends, Chateau Squalor would have been seen in its true mucky colours. My girlfriend Caroline organised her painter to come and do several rooms, bits of ceiling, bits of wall that I hadn't even noticed had gone all scabby. Vera cleaned out all my cupboards. I went down to the garden centre and had instant window boxes done to replace the petrified forest that normally sits outside my bedroom window, loved only by the sparrows who use it as a dust bath.

When I mentioned the problem to Marti Caine, with whom I was appearing in 'New Faces', she immediately said, 'I'll come round and clean for you'. She's the absolute opposite of me – she adores cleaning and scrubbing, wearing rubber gloves and picking tiny bits of fluff out of holes, getting every single thing out of cupboards, taking things down and washing them. I think she's nuts but it seems to be therapy for her. So two days before filming, she rang up and said, 'It's tomorrow, isn't it, that I'm coming to clean your kitchen?' I felt dreadful. 'No, you can't possibly, don't be silly.' But she said, 'I've got all me stuff with me, me carpet cleaner, me shampoo and everything!'

I said, 'Oh I'm so sorry, I've already organised this, really Marti . . .'.

Then she said, 'But it would be such a great *pleasure.*'

I suggested we meet for lunch instead. So we had lunch and then went to Harrods and bought a million flowers for disguise – if you've got piles of flowers all over the place, no one notices the clutter – and carted them back home in a taxi.

Marti then got out a carrier bag in which she had her cleaning kit. She changed into leggings and a long shirt and pulled on her rubber gloves to the amazement of Vera, who she then told, 'I'm at your disposal. We're partners in grime. You tell me what to do.'

Vera was utterly gobsmacked. Marti went into the kitchen and she cleaned every cup, every saucer, every shelf, every old spice jar, every old bit of fungus, the fridge, wiped every surface, she did the lot. When she'd finished that, she turned her attention to four upright chairs in the living room, good pine chairs but I'd never really liked the fabric that covered the bases. So I'd bought this fabric about six years ago, that exactly matched the sofa, to cover the base of the chairs. But I'd never got round to actually putting them on the chairs. I had the fabric neatly folded up in the living room so I could look at it, which I did once or twice a day. And every time I looked at it, it made me angry.

'Do you want these chairs covered?' said Marti – and she did it in half an hour. She got a hammer, whipped out the seats, cut out four squares of fabric, covered them and whipped it all back together. No upholstery tacks, nothing. Brilliant.

The flat looked perfect by the end of the day. There was just one more thing – the fridge was empty. So I thought I'd rise at dawn and go and get half a chicken and those things that normal people have in their fridge.

But unfortunately I went to a party that night. And as I was wearing my Behaving Badly Frock, I ended up being dragged through the shrubbery by someone. All I could think, as I staggered home at five in the morning, was, 'My God, the cameras will be here at ten'.

I woke up with that fallen-down-a-mineshaft feeling and as I dragged myself into the kitchen I realised there were some marks on the wall and the only way to get rid of them was to hang two pictures over them. So I got up on my wobbly kitchen steps and knocked in a picture hook – and a huge bit of plaster fell down. I did it again and the same thing happened. As I tried to knock in more and more hooks, the whole wall was being destroyed.

I was so shaky I could hardly stand, but I was too stupefied to work out that if I left it for an hour and a half, I might feel a bit better and there would still be time to do it. I had just two hooks left and all I could think was: I've gotta do it.

Those two hooks and the pictures covering the marks and the masses of holes in the plaster are there still, a reminder that a hangover is not a cue to hang pictures.

After that, there was no way I could go shopping for fridge fodder. So when Loyd Grossman eventually opened the refrigerator door, there was a bottle of pink champagne, a bottle of Diet Coke, a bottle of skimmed milk and a half bottle of Muscadet. And that was it. As

Loyd entered the kitchen he commented, 'This looks like the canteen of a Martian space lab – obviously the home of a serious cook.' Anyone with more than three wooden spoons is a serious cook on that show but I still wondered how he was going to deal with the fridge contents. When he opened the door he said without hesitating, 'Clearly, she's on a non-solid diet at the moment.' I think it must have been the word 'diet' that gave away my identity – or perhaps it was the preponderance of pink?

The things that furnish a place are, I think, books, music and flowers. I don't notice the rest.

I used to have to have someone clean up because I used to be allergic to dust. Can you imagine somebody scruffy, who's allergic to dust? Now I don't even notice it. And if I did, I wouldn't do anything about it – after all, it's only me that's got to live with it.

Of course, I mostly hang my clothes on the floor. Or on the exercise bike that's gone ninety-seven kilometres in eight years. My built-in wardrobe is collapsing, the sliding doors are falling off and I can't get anyone to mend them. So they just hang there and I heave them apart when I need to get something in or out. That cupboard looks as if everything in the world that is pink, black or white has been melted and poured into it in a big congealed mass. Its floor is covered in old shoes, old clothes, carrier bags and things I don't know what to do with. I really ought to clear it out. I have tried and Vera has offered to help. But I get very cross when people try to organise me. 'I'll come round one day and we'll do it together', she said. But I did it with such ill grace because I didn't want to do it and didn't want anyone to do it for me, either. You'd think I'd be grateful but obviously I must like it like that.

In fact I think I must like everything like that, the dressing table is a complete mess too and even Vera has completely given up trying to tidy it. It's littered with bits of make-up, bits of jewellery, old tissues, safety pins, bits of sewing, bills, odd notes, coins, broken hair brushes, heated rollers and all the jewellery is on top of a chest of drawers instead of in its boxes. I never know what I've lost and what I haven't lost. And I don't know what's in the chest of drawers – I haven't opened it in years.

On the floor underneath the dressing table is a mountain of shoes, mostly pink, and boots – I suppose there are about twenty or thirty pairs under there, all mixed up. These are ostensibly the shoes I wear most and they just lie there looking like a Lost and Found shoe department. I sometimes think all the lost shoes in the world end up in my bedroom. (Where then are all of mine, I wonder?)

There is some design element to all this chaos, however. My splendidly co-ordinated bedroom furniture, for instance, was planned as a result of a very good lunch in St John's Wood High Street. It was there I saw this dragged green rattan furniture which looked very Caribbean and immediately appealed to me. So I went in and asked, 'Can you do the green in pink?' And they said, 'Yes, just tell us what shade.' So I got the dressing table, the bed, the bedside chair, the dressing table, all in the precise pink I fancied. It doesn't exactly look Caribbean any more but I love it as my only successful piece of interior planning.

The fact that the bed collapses from time to time is another issue. It has also started squeaking – even when there is nothing particular going on in it. The first time this happened I woke up in the middle of the night by myself and rolled over and it squeaked. And every time I turned over, it squeaked and squeaked and squeaked.

Eventually I got up, went into the kitchen and found a tin of Three-in-One oil left behind by the last workman but one. So there I was, at nine o'clock in the morning, in my Marks and Spencer's pink satin nightshirt, oiling the bed, when the doorbell rang. It turned out to be an ex-lover. 'Quick, quick, can I come up?' he said over the intercom, 'I've got to talk to you.'

I did let him up in the end, fondly thinking that in my pink nightshirt and a pair of dark glasses to hide the lack of make-up I looked a bit like Cybill Shepherd from 'Moonlighting', in her part as Maddy Hayes. In fact I looked more like Tubby Hayes.

Amazingly it was quite a tussle to get him from the hall into the living room rather than the bedroom. It must have been the can of Three-in-One that did it – perhaps he had a thing about DIY women?

If only I *did* have a talent for fixing, redecorating or refurbishing I would not have had to endure the saga of having my bathroom repainted. Indeed I tried to pretend it wasn't happening by borrowing a fortune to get in the professionals and going away for a week to let them get on with it. It was the week before Christmas and when I got back, as I was climbing the steps on a late Friday afternoon, I saw a note pinned to my door. It was from the people upstairs and it said, 'Before you go into your flat, please read this.' As I pulled it off the front door, the paint came away with the Sellotape and then I started to read, 'I'm afraid we had a slight accident . . .'.

Their washing machine had overflowed and my bathroom ceiling had come down. All the newly decorated bathroom was in a state of collapse with rubble all over the floor.

When they had come down to see the damage, they smelled gas. So they called the Gas Board who said there was a leak and turned off all my gas. So I had no heating, no hot water, no bathroom – and it was the Friday before Christmas. Everything had stopped. I didn't get the gas back till nearly New Year.

That has put me off decorating the flat. I know it wouldn't have happened if the place had been in the scrubby old squalid state it usually is.

And I'm so bad with workmen. They say when you have any work done you have got to be there to hammer them. I always go away so I can avoid them.

I went to Montserrat for Christmas five years ago when

my marvellous kitchen was supposed to be put in. For weeks beforehand I'd had all the kitchen crockery under the sofa in the living room, piled up out of the way. It was supposed to be ready when I got back. As I climbed the stairs I thought, 'Maybe it won't be quite finished – but that's all right.'

Then, as I opened the living room door I saw that the whole room was piled with rubbish. There were bags of cement on the carpet, tools everywhere, plans – and an open tin of golden syrup that certainly wasn't mine. In the kitchen there was nothing, just bare plaster walls, not even a point to put a kettle into. There wasn't a single unit, not a sink, not a shelf. There was a fridge in my bedroom, unplugged and filled with rotting food.

Every time I try to do something, I get a disaster. What am I doing wrong? What's wrong with *them*?

A live-in handyman is the obvious answer. But have you ever seen the sort of men who hang out in DIY shops? Nothing to raise a woman's spirit level there, I can tell you. When I say I like a man who's good with his hands, it's not woodwork I have in mind. And though I do like my pictures well-hung, I prefer a man that way even more.

I've never really minded men who don't do housework because I don't do it myself. But on the other hand if they want to be tidy, I'll always lift my feet so they can Hoover underneath.

Big ends and bumper fun

You can tell people's characters by their cars. I once met a millionaire at a very smart dinner party in Putney and I thought him great fun and he fancied me – but then I saw his car. It was sitting out there in the moonlight, a gold XJS with initial number plates.

As I pottered round to the passenger side I exclaimed, 'What *is* this?' And he replied, 'It's my motor.' He said it without pronouncing the 't'.

'*Gold!*' I said, 'It's disgusting. And *initial number plates*! You should be ashamed of yourself.' He thought I was joking.

To get into the front seat took the physical skills of Jane Fonda. And once in, I lay quite flat. Not very enticing.

'What are you doing down there?' he asked in some amazement. 'I don't want anyone to see me', I piped up from the depths. 'Well, as it's two o'clock in the morning you should be all right', he said through slightly tight lips. I honestly thought he'd got that car out for the evening as a joke.

But gold Jags aren't my only hate – there are plenty of other horrors I'd like to see off the road. I hate men who drive red cars, usually salesmen in yuppie red XR3s with a jacket hanging in the window. Particularly when they have a woman with them and they're alongside you at traffic lights: they practically burn up a year's supply of rubber shooting away when the lights change. It's pathetic. And you will notice on the motorway, it's always men in red cars who have to be in the outside lane, going faster and faster and faster.

I was once carved up round the back of Fleet Street while looking for a place to park. There I was, stopped at a little junction waiting for another car to pass before I turned right, when the car behind me gently ran into the back of me. The guy stuck his head out the window and yelled, 'It's your own bloody fault. Why didn't you move off?'

'Because there's a car coming – dipstick.' He then shot around the outside of me and roared off, shouting as he went, 'Fuck orf.' It wasn't the fuck, it was the way he pronounced the orf that got to me. He was one of those types, in his forties – greasy-headed and think they're too grand to wash their hair.

He was obviously looking for a parking place as well, so I got in tight behind him, nose-to-tail and we went round and round and round. At one point he stopped and obviously thought I'd go away – but I pulled up right behind him and waited for him to get out. But he didn't – he was too scared.

After about five minutes I realised I'd have to go or I'd be late for the office. So I got out of my car and locked it. He, meanwhile, was sitting in his car with the window up, looking down and pretending to fiddle with his keys. I knocked on the window and he pretended not to hear. I said, 'I know you're not deaf, I know you can hear every word I'm saying. You're pretending you can't. You're only brave in the car, aren't you? Only a big man in the car? You think you can carve people up and drive badly and get away with it? Well, let me tell you, if that gives you pleasure, good luck. But may I make one suggestion: if you're going to shout smart-arse comments out of the window, at least look the part. Just wash your hair occasionally.' And I walked off. He just sat there twitching like the pillock he was. It didn't give me that much satisfaction but it did make me wonder what makes a man behave like that behind a wheel? And he was not un-usual, as any woman driver can attest.

If there are drivers I can't stand, there are also cars I'd like to kick – like Volvos. They're so sensible and they're always driven by smug people who drive either very, very carefully or very fast in the knowledge that if they crash they've got a protective steel cage around them. Too bad for any poor little ancient rust-bucket that might get in their way.

Then there is the BMW. If I'm driving through Lon-don and I'm behind a black BMW driven by a yuppie talking on a car phone at the same time, I have an insatiable urge to ram it. I have to restrain myself with the thought that I am not at the dodgems at the fair-ground. Because I just want to go *BOOM*. Even though it would damage my car.

I also dislike all Fords, especially Cortinas with the old nodding dogs in the back window. I have an aversion too, to seeing Garfield stuck by the paws to the inside of car windows. I think I preferred furry dice. But generally cars full of fluffy toys and dangling objects make me want to smash their windows. Nor do I warm towards people who have those signs on their bumper or back wind-screen, 'If you can read this you're too close' or 'Wind-surfers do it standing up' or 'Back off baby on board'.

Funny how you never see that sort of thing on Bentleys or Rolls Royces – yet I think the Roller is so deeply naff I'd never want to have one. I enjoy a ride in one occa-sionally but I don't want to own one. I just don't lust after other people's cars. I either think, 'That's nice', or 'Christ, how could they? How could they buy a yellow car? Or a blue car?'

Another prize-winner in the most loathed car category is the Suzuki jeep, most commonly driven by a certain kind of woman – an over-tanned, under-brained bimbo. She thinks she's on safari – in Knightsbridge! Well, I suppose many of them *are* big-game hunting when you think of it.

As a driver I'm a creature of habit and I don't like very sensible cars. The first car I ever bought was a black Renault 5 and I've kept buying the same ever since.

The least sensible Renault 5 I ever had was a convertible, a ridiculous choice because Renault don't make convertibles. This was a custom-built thing I bought when it was a year old. The roof didn't quite fit and it was like travelling in a hair-dryer – but I loved it. It was a beautiful shape with the top down. I called it The Pram.

It was not its finest hour when it got caught in a torrential downpour at two o'clock one morning. I couldn't bring myself to go downstairs and put its top on, so by daybreak it was four inches deep in water. I had to bale it out with a beaker then swab it down with towels before I could go to work, sitting on a black plastic binliner.

That was the first week I stood in for Derek Jameson on his Radio Two show and he had handed me his pass for the BBC car park like someone handing on the Olympic flame. But my arrival each day, perched on the bin liner and desperately trying to avoid damp patches on the bum, was less than glorious, as the car took over a week to dry out. If I'd left it as it was, I could've kept goldfish in it – or even trout, or salmon.

I look after my car the same way I look after my shoes. I can't understand those people who say, 'Why do you have a black car? They get dirty so quickly, you must have to wash it so often.'

No I don't. I just leave it till I notice it's dirty. Then, when I remember, I take it down to my favourite car-wash, which has big pink fluffy rollers. It's wonderful to sit in your car with all this pinkness whooshing around you.

My latest car was only a few weeks' old when it began to look like a giant ashtray, despite the fact it had actually been cleaned twice. This, of course, had no effect on the inside. Its interior went from shiny to shitty in a matter of moments, filled with old bits of paper and empty peanut and raisin packets. It looked so awful, even I noticed it. This was mainly due to the layer of pine needles carpeting it. Every Christmas I buy a blue spruce, a growing pine tree. And every year I release it into a friend's garden in Surrey. But this time I released it too late, not till May, and when I lifted it into the car enough pine needles to carpet a forest fell everywhere. Not that I mind them – well, not enough to do anything about them, certainly.

I also wouldn't ever do anything about the mechanics of my car. Its inside workings are as incomprehensible to me as people who buy Max Bygraves' records. I do know the principles of changing a tyre but there's no way I'm ever going to do it. I'd hate to begin to learn.

I'm now a brilliant driver because I do it sober – this is a cautionary tale. Not only did I once habitually drink and drive but I used to drink and drive a lot. Like so many people, I used to think, 'I'm never going to get caught, everybody does it'. I used to drive home automatically from the pub and not remember how I got home. I'd wake up in the morning and rush – or rather stagger with a hangover – to the front window and there would be the car immaculately parked, better than normal. And I'd think, 'This is all right.' Because I did it so often it was part of life. Looking back on it makes me feel dreadful.

I'm a bit like a reformed smoker now: I want to change everybody else. And if I've had one glass of wine with lunch, I won't drive for the rest of the day. Which doesn't happen very often as I don't see the point of a glass of wine anyway. Consequently, if I'm not driving, I'll be drinking.

The turning point came after I'd been to a film preview of 'Educating Rita' and when you're lucky enough to go to a preview, there is always plenty of free booze and crisps, you sit back and sip and munch while you watch the film. I loved the film so much I was in an *extremely* good mood, knocking back the white wine and roaring

Hard to believe this lump of dough in a petticoat is me

As a two-year-old I was kept on a tight rein, most people reckon that as a forty-two-year-old I should have been kept on an even tighter one

Lurching around and needing support at eighteen months, a sign of things to come?

Below: Three feet tall and weighing thirty pounds, I was ready for my first day at school

Above: Those hated sensible shoes

In a school production of Jane Eyre (I'm second from the left). My only line was 'dinner time must come some time' – appropriately enough

Aged six, with Hamish. Obsessed with my weight even at that age I told my mother to 'send this to Grandpa to let him see I'm *not* fat'

The 'bitch on the box', complete with box

The only essential companion for a happy
Christmas – a bottle of champagne

Below: It took a lot of cocktails to get me to do it but here's proof of my epic thirty-foot topless dive

Next page: Me and my perfect car, a customised Renault 5 convertible

with laughter. Afterwards I went to the pub. And then I started to drive home.

Coming up Regent Street, just past Broadcasting House, there's a slight bend in the road. I managed to negotiate it – but then I somehow forgot to straighten up and went slamming into a parked car which hit the car in front of that, which hit the car in front of that, which hit the car. . . .

Fortunately there were no people involved and I wasn't hurt at all, just bruised. But I just sat there stunned, thinking, 'I don't believe it'. I didn't know what to do about it. I just thought, 'Jeez I'm drunk' – and I wanted to get home.

What I should have done, I know now, is leave a note on the windscreen with my name on it and leg it off somewhere else. But I wasn't thinking well at all. I switched on the engine which coughed into action, then reversed with an enormous grinding of metal and started to drive home.

I only got a few hundred yards up the road when there was a blue flashing light behind me and the sound of a very loud siren. I discovered the reason they were stopping me was that I had no back lights – the crash had put the electrics out. And then when the cops came round the front of the car it was like three lemons going up at once: they'd cracked the jackpot. They had seen the wreckage back down the road so they put two and two together and arrested me. I was taken to the station, a most appalling experience – and waited for the doctor to come and take a blood sample. After that, they give you a card telling you the garage where your car has been taken. Then they shove you out into the middle of the night. There you are, you have to get a taxi home – and you're a criminal.

You can't sleep properly because you know you're going to lose your licence. Then, in my case, the doorbell rang at eight in the morning as I lay in bed thinking, 'God, I must be the worst person in the world'. I was wracked with guilt and also wracked with headache. I was so hungover when the bell rang that I picked up the phone and said hello. When I realised it was the door I picked up the intercom and a voice said, 'Is that Nina Miss-Cow? PC One-Four-Nine 'ere, I've come about the incident last night.'

So there I was in my dressing gown feeling like the wrath of God and the wreck of the Hesperus rolled into one, standing there staring at the policeman's feet on the carpet. They were huge, classic police feet in shoes with toecaps and the ends curled up like British Rail sandwiches. We then had a conversation which, if you heard it in a sitcom, you would never believe that people really talked like that.

We were at cross purposes and I couldn't understand what he was talking about, so I kept repeating what he said. 'What is it?' I began.

'I've come about your lost property, madam.'

'Lost property?'

'Yes, madam, your lost property.'

'My lost property?'

'Yes, madam, your lost property is in Marylebone Police Station.'

'Marylebone Police Station?' I muttered, puzzled, because I hadn't a clue which police station I'd been taken to.

'Yes, madam, Marylebone Police Station.'

'*Marylebone Police Station?*'

'Yes, madam, your lost property is in Marylebone Police Station.'

'*My lost property! What lost property?*'

He replied, 'Your radiator grill.'

It must have fallen off in the collision. At that point I burst out laughing and told him, 'Listen, if you can fit it into a carrier bag, it's yours. But thank you very much all the same.'

That was the only funny bit. When you go to court and have your licence taken away it's no joke. I lost it for twelve months and it was a hard lesson. It's such a loss of freedom. I know I'm lucky to be able to afford to run a car and I was lucky in that I don't live in the middle of the country. At least when you live in Central London finding taxis is not difficult. But it was still enough to teach me not to do that kind of thing any more.

When I think back to my drunk driving I feel quite sick. I could have mown down the whole population of Britain – might have done a few people a favour but it makes my blood run cold. When I'm drunk I'm not capable of being in charge of a pair of stiletto heels or roller skates, let alone a car. When you think about it: if you're about to fall over, there's no way you can keep a car straight.

I once interviewed Rita Coolidge who was married to Kris Kristofferson in his heavy drinking days when he used to wake up every morning and have what he called The Old Sock, which was a vodka and grapefruit juice. She said that when he was drunk he drove perfectly – but when he was sober, he kept hitting the kerb because he couldn't do it. I never got that bad.

The car that lost me my licence was a car I hated (and a rare departure from my usual Renault 5s), a blue Ford Escort which is a cheese salesman's car as far as I'm concerned. It had an unsightly stain on the passenger seat which worried me for a long time until the previous owner assured me that it was takeaway curry. But I always hated that car and I'm quite convinced that if it had been a car that I loved, I wouldn't have crashed it.

The car of my dreams is a pink car but it would just be too high profile – somebody would be bound to slash it. But if I was very rich, a pink car I'd have. I saw a Porsche the exact colour of my pink watch-strap and I wondered, 'Would I really want that? Yeah, childish, but I'm afraid I would'.

Because I don't have pets and don't have children I become attached to my car – though perhaps not in quite the same way. My car is not just a piece of equipment like it is for a lot of people. It's *my* car therefore it means more to me than to other people. The convertible was ludicrous because it was like having a hyperactive child or a dog that bit people. People would say, 'How can you put up with it? How do you cope?' And I'd think, 'Because it's *my* car'. It eventually got to the stage where a vandal had slashed the roof and the back strut had collapsed so I could only drive it with the top down because the roof wouldn't go up. Then it would break down on the motorway. Then it got a puncture, parking.

Parking! Those high rise carparks! How do people survive those without going to psychiatrists afterwards? You're going round and round and round with a ticket between your teeth, going up and up and up. You become quite demented by the time you get to the top. I came back to the car once – and I had a puncture. It had acquired a puncture sitting in the car park. That was the moment I faced up to divorce. I looked at that collapsed tyre and decided, 'This is it, car, I love you dearly but frankly, this is the end'. So I traded it in on a new Renault 5 with sunshine roof, a fabric top that goes from front to back and makes it *almost* a convertible.

Within two weeks I had broken the sun visor. I slammed the roof shut, crunch, when the visor was up. It's very depressing when you have something new like that and you want it to be pristine and new forever. And now it won't ever be. A classic Myskow-mobile.

I learned to drive in the country, but though I know how to drive through snow and mud and all that stuff I'm very scathing about country drivers. I am used to driving in traffic and I can't stand people who pootle along. There's nothing worse than being behind a pootling car. Then you pass it and see it's a woman driver and you think, 'How embarrassing! How could she! It's women like that who give us all a bad name'.

I also have a theory about drivers who wear hats: they never seem able to turn left or right without hogging the whole road. Which always give me a strong urge to drive up their boots.

I didn't have a car for the first year I was in London. I did it deliberately so that I could learn all the taxi routes. Now I know all the little back-alley ways and I just put my foot down and go. (I never went by underground because I get claustrophobic, I'd rather go on a bus – except I'd rather die than go on a bus.)

As a result of all this, I drive like a taxi driver. The only difference is, I don't have right-wing views. I'm not constantly forcing my admiration of Maggie Thatcher on some poor sod in the back seat.

Shop till you drop

In my passport, it says occupation: journalist – something I've never quite believed. In my heart it says Shopper. It's just written there; possibly the S is a dollar sign.

You know how great actors always want to snuff it in mid-performance on stage? Well, my ideal way to go is collapsed under the weight of carrier bags in the beauty department of Harvey Nichols. There I would feel totally at rest, at peace: okay, I've done it, that's it. Goodnight Vienna, I'm going home.

Somehow once you start shopping you never want to stop. And it's not the big things, it's the frittery things that are such a pleasure to buy. You start on a bit of make-up, then maybe a belt or a handbag or a magazine. There's nothing quite like the satisfaction of barrelling into a taxi outside Harvey Nicks at the top of Sloane Street with these carrier bags so heavy your fingers become like sausages with the plastic handles cutting into you. You're carrying so many bags you can barely get through the door of the taxi and you just sit back there, sinking into the back seat of the cab all spread round with parcels. There's just such complete joy, getting it home and taking all these new things out. I just love it – therefore the times when I haven't been able to shop, I've been really appalling and felt totally deprived.

I'm also a menace if I go shopping with somebody because I can make anybody spend money. I don't know what the opposite of a minder is, but that's what I am. I've made my friend Caroline buy Yves St Laurent jackets she never even wanted. I've made other people buy clothes they wouldn't have dreamed about. The only thing in my defence is, they've never regretted it – or perhaps they wouldn't dare tell me.

A lot of people say they can't stand shopping, which I can never understand. There is only one sort of shopping I loathe: shopping in the supermarket for everyday things. One of the great things about being single and living in London in particular is that you don't *have* to do Sainsburys on a Saturday morning, not unless you *want* to run over children with a trolley. Where I live there are places where you can shop at ten or eleven at night, you can just pick up what you want and there are no ankle-biters under foot, snapping at your heels and whining at their mums.

I used to be thrilled by shopping abroad and bringing home all those exotic things with foreign labels. But these days my most extravagant foreign buys are likely to be Turkish tampax, Dutch deodorant or Italian aspirin. Things like antique rugs, silver trinkets and native artefacts are out of the question since my credit cards got taken away. I've been totally curtailed in that area because of my plasticlessness: I can't run up international mega-debts like I used to. And that's a real pain – the only upside is, I don't have any hassle with customs. Oh to have Something to Declare – but once I get all that back in action you won't be able to see me for excess luggage.

It's sad that shopping is so tied up with money. I don't know why they don't just give me things to make me happy. 'Make this woman go away – give her something pink.' When the missionaries went out to the savages, they used to dangle beads and shiny objects to keep them happy – they could do this to me, too.

Pink things in shops are irresistible to me. I've tried to

get out of it but I certainly buy things *because* they're pink. If lavatory cleaner came in pink bottles I could sit and look at it all day. I only write on pink note pads, I carry my cosmetics round in big pink bags, my workout clothes are pink – even my loo seat is made of pink padded plastic. (It's American and came from one of those hi-tech shops in Covent Garden. When I spotted it I thought: that's for me. I've never had a padded loo seat before, it's very comfortable. And the pink cheers you up.)

My pink cigarette fetish started in New York when I was there to see The Police play Madison Square Garden for the first time. I was staying at a hotel on the corner of Fifth Avenue and I'd seen '42nd Street' the night before and was practically dancing down the street – Fifth Avenue always makes me feel like that. It was January and freezing and on the corner of 55th and Fifth I spied a very grand tobacconist called Nat Sherman's which had in the window a display of 'Nat Sherman's Fantasia.' These were cigarettes seven and a half inches long which came in all different colours and, blissfully, shocking pink. I went and asked if they did them in big boxes and they asked, 'Would madam care to try one?'

'No thanks, I don't smoke, I only hold.'

Americans can't take that sort of thing. I could see them backing off, ('We've got a loony in the shop, Bert.') I could see them reaching with their feet for the alarm button.

But I bought five boxes of ten and went off to the concert in one of those silly limos where you climb in and try to get the television to work but you can't because of the Manhattan skyscrapers. And you've got a vodka and tonic in your hand and had quite a bit to drink so that when you get out of the limo at a party somewhere downtown you practically fall out on to the pavement just managing not to spill your drink. Then you have to extricate your heel from the grating before you finally totter into the party.

This time was no different. So I got into the crowded room, got out the pink cigarettes, lit up and stood there like the Statue of Liberty, holding the thing between two fingers in the air. No smoking it, of course. Sting then came over to me and said, 'You don't smoke.'

'No. I'm not smoking, I'm just holding it.'

'Can I have one?'

'*You* don't smoke.'

'So neither of us does.'

'But I bought them – why do you want one?'

'You're upstaging me.'

'Aha, I will give you a cigarette if you'll play the last scene from *Now Voyager* with me.'

It's a Bette Davis movie with Paul Henreid where he puts two cigarettes in his mouth, lights them both and gives her one. They are standing in front of a window and both drag deeply at them, then he says to her very soulfully, 'But will you be happy?' And she looks up at him and says, 'Why should I ask for the moon when I have the stars?' And the camera pans upwards into the starry sky.

So in the middle of this party we did it and it was hilarious. That set the tone, really. Ever since, I've felt obliged to ask anyone who ever goes to New York to bring me back some pink cigarettes.

Pink is a habit that's made clothes shopping really easy for me as well. Because I only wear pink with black or white, that cuts out a whole lot of crap. I don't even look at other things.

That's one way of getting straight to the goodies. You walk into a shop and there they are: anything pink I look at. For instance, I cannot pass a pink shoe. I lose count of the pairs I own and I lose the shoes as well.

I lost a pink shoe in a disco in Nottingham where I was making a series of Anglia programmes. I got anglia and anglia when I discovered the shoe was missing. It was the last of the series and we all went to a big disco afterwards, about ten of us. I kicked my shoes off under the table where we were sitting and went and danced. We danced and danced till the place was closing then we went upstairs and had more champagne with the manager. And when we came back down to go home, somebody had nicked one of my shoes. I can't imagine they had taken it as a drinking vessel – not after they had seen the foot that went inside it.

With me and shoes, I'm almost into the Imelda Marcos league. I have a 1940s postcard someone once gave me, which sums up my attitude to shoes. It says, 'She was a shopaholic. She could not contain her crazed lust for shoes. Nothing could satisfy her.' It shows a woman in one of those daft Forties hats sitting in a shop trying on a shoe and the salesman is kneeling in front of her holding up another one. He's looking at her and saying, 'Go ahead, lick it.' (Not that I'm into shoes in that sort of way – I just love them for what they are. Like Belgian fresh cream chocolate truffles, you simply can't have too many of them.) On holiday in Bali I lost one Reebok and spent two weeks searching in vain for a one-legged Balinese to give the other one to.

But though I may buy a lot of them I'm not very good at cleaning them. I just wear them dirty or throw them away. My shoes just lie in the bottom of the wardrobe, uncared for and unloved.

I'm as hard on all my other clothes as I am on my shoes. If I iron a pair of trousers, I melt holes in them. The state of my iron says it all: the flex is completely shredded. So if I see anything that's pink with a label that says Do Not Iron, that's for me.

I have even more pairs of earrings than I have shoes. And I lose them even more regularly. I lose them on holiday or being dragged into shrubbery – in fact losing earrings has become a euphemism for bonking. 'How many earrings did you lose?' they ask when I come back from holiday.

I absolutely adore great big earrings. I've probably got

about forty pairs – or half pairs. Otherwise, I don't really like jewellery. Giant clonking diamonds don't really suit me, I suppose because I've never been able to afford them and also I can't imagine myself wearing them. I know people who have to wear the Cartier or the Rolex watch, but I never notice things like that. I notice fabulous jewellery that's interesting, but not glittery jewellery. Elton John, on the morning the *Sun* paid him £1 million libel damages and said SORRY ELTON all over the front page, went to Cartier and bought an enormous sapphire ring. The stone was the size of a small Brussels sprout. It was forty-two-and-a-half carats and I'd never seen anything like it close up. He could barely pick up his chopsticks to eat at the swish Chinese celebration party that evening. But I wouldn't want to own that. How could you put your tights on?

Real jewellery doesn't appeal to me, perhaps because I know I'd lose it. I'd drop it or give it away when I was drunk. I don't see the point of it.

Status symbols are lost on me. I really can't stand that whole thing of wearing an item like a little badge that says, 'Look at me, I'm wearing a Rolex watch, I belong to the club. I can afford this, so aren't I terrific?'

Vuitton handbags are the worst status symbol ever: a) they're brown, and b) they're plastic. I'd rather have a carrier bag from The Body Shop. Vuitton bags are naff and nouveau. In a way the French get away with them because it's their thing but everyone else just looks tatty with them.

I would also like to stamp out the kind of people who move fifteen miles out of London and instantly buy a Barbour and green wellies. The only possible accessory to those is a gun – held by me. I hate that pretence of country squiredom. Who wants to look that hearty, anyway?

I have a card which says, 'I shop therefore I am.' I find that the spirits dwindle if you don't shop. And if you're depressed, nothing can actually lift you faster than a good shop. Better than cake, champagne or even chocolate. You just need to go out and buy a little something that you like. Nothing expensive, but just buying one little thing that you like can do wonders. So does finding some little thing for someone else. I love buying things for other people, seeing something and thinking, that's perfect for so-and-so. That's really the *best* kind of shopping, especially when it's followed by seeing somebody's face as they open it and knowing you've got exactly the right thing.

You've got to be dressed right for shopping, too. If you're going to be trying things on you don't want to be wearing stuff that you have to unbutton and heave yourself in and out of and trainers that you have to untie. There's nothing more boring than dragging clothes on and off till you're so hot and bothered you can't actually buy anything. You've got to be in the right gear to do it.

Apart from the question of comfort and speed, there is the appalling challenge of the communal changing room. Is there anyone who could like them? Only a lesbian could love a communal changing room. However confident you are in the way you look and what you're doing, you can't possibly go into one of those things and find it a pleasurable experience. You see people getting into a corner, trying to get a tiny bit of privacy, to hide their greying knickers and holey tights or the white flab around their middles.

The only thing worse than that is what passes for a private changing room in one of those jeans shops. They have those saloon bar doors with slats and you're never quite sure that you can't be seen through the slats. The doors don't quite meet – and they only come down to knee-level.

Anywhere you try on jeans should have enough space so you can lie on the floor. It's a simple equation – you have to lie on the floor to pull them up. All jeans shops ought to have a place where you can lie on the floor and nobody can see you lying there. Jeans are things you have to wriggle into like a worm.

Have you heard about those Japanese hotels where they stack you in modules, like little sleeping pods? Well, you could have jean-changing pods where you didn't have to be upright, you'd just slide in and pull the jeans on. That would be much more sensible.

Shopping when you're big can be a nightmare. There are shops you wouldn't even think of going into, upmarket underwear shops for instance. I once went into a shop called Leather Rat and was looking at the skirts when the assistant said, 'We've got nothing in here to fit you.' And she was probably right. But I just thought, 'I will never, even if I get skeletal, buy anything from your shop.' And every time I drive past, I still blow them a raspberry.

Victoria Wood once wrote a brilliant sketch about shopping, with Julie Walters as the shop assistant and Victoria Wood as the customer. When Victoria asked, 'Do you have anything in a size 14?' Julie replied, 'We don't serve obese people in here, they sweat on the wallpaper.' When you think about it, those cubicles are always so small, it's probably true.

How do I choose what's right for me? In the old days, if it was pink and voluminous, it was mine. I spent years and years finding ways of covering up, different variations on the tent. I got very clever at it because it's very hard to dress when you're bigger. There are some things that make you look absolutely normal and all right and others that are completely disastrous. Other people don't know how awful it is.

Casual dressing has always been difficult for me. Because I've always had to dress very carefully to disguise my shape, I can only really do Very Dressed Up and Very Smart. It's harder to dress casually and look good if you're bigger. Can you imagine Claire Rayner in leggings?

Underwear is much more fun to shop for now. Years

ago I was a 36C which, in the Sixties, was severely
limiting when shopping for bras. Anything in a C cup
was always huge, white, and underwired with four great
hooks at the back. I longed to be able to wear something
with one hook at the back but they didn't make them for
girls my size. I felt deprived for many years because I
couldn't get the kind of bra a man might want to tear off.
He'd have to be into tearing telephone books to have the
strength to get to grips with mine.

The secret of shopping must be in knowing what you
want (and knowing how to get the money to pay for it –
but that's another problem). Some things just leap off the
rails and say, 'Buy me'. Anything that makes you look
better makes you feel good. If it makes you feel so good
you feel bad, that's the one.

Shopping has been two hundred per cent more fun
since I lost weight and got down to a size 12. I was never
more than a 16, but try to find anything you'd be seen
dead or alive in that's a size 16. I must say that the first
time I went into a shop in a January sale and saw a black
French pigskin skirt with a matching blouse, size 14 *with
a loose waistband*, I just thought it was labelled wrongly.
Although I knew I'd lost weight I still thought there was a
mistake. I asked the salesgirl who assured me the size was
right and offered to get a smaller one in from another
branch.

I went back the next day and got very gingerly into the
size 12 and thought of the number of times I'd got that
defeated feeling when I pulled something halfway up and
realised it wasn't going to go any further. And I got this
thing on and got to the stage where it might have stuck –
and it did up perfectly. I was so excited, I leaped out from
behind the curtain and shrieked, 'Look! Look, it fits.' I
was dancing round the shop and practically rushing out
into the street, calling, 'Look, this is a size 12, I can fit
into it!'

I hate wearing anything on my legs and avoid stockings

and tights as much as possible (except for three weeks after my legs have been waxed when covering them becomes imperative). I suppose I choose tights for ease and stockings for fun. The trouble with shorter skirts is that you can't wear stockings.

At one stage when the mini was around the first time, I was quite slim because I was on diet pills. (I was so high you practically had to scrape me off the ceiling – but I was thinner.) I was fashion editor of *Jackie* magazine, if you can imagine, and I had a dress that looked like a French blue rugby shirt which had a white pocket and little hanky sticking out of it – and the skirt was so short it had matching knickers. I wore this through the centre of London still wishing desperately that I had lovely legs. What pissed me off was that the ugliest girls, as long as they were thin and had long legs and could grow their hair and dye it blonde, looked fabulous. The mini was the time when ugly girls with good legs came into their own. It was a good disguise because nobody looked at their pig's-bottom faces, all you could see was leg and blonde hair and nothing else seemed to matter. I remember thinking it was terribly unfair.

It was an era when *everybody* was wearing minis – you saw some terrible sights but they seemed to get away with it. The one thing that seemed to cheer me up then was that doctors said if you wore minis in the middle of winter your thighs would get fat – I prayed for an early winter!

But for the brief time I was able to wear these quite short skirts I felt emancipated for the first time. Until I was forty I went through life wearing clothes that covered me up rather than clothes to enhance my figure. (Mind you, there was nothing – or rather, there was too much – to enhance.) Somehow I never thought of coping with it the way some big girls do, by letting everything hang out of the front window. I suppose the theory is: if you're fat you've probably got big boobs so why not wear low-cut dresses. Like wearing the mini skirt if you've got skinny legs. But I never had the confidence to do it.

This summer I can just about cope with the mini: if you live long enough you nearly always get a second go at everything.

There aren't that many disasters in my wardrobe because after a while you get to know what you like. The clothes I buy I really love and I wear them and wear them and don't mind how often.

I also have to have a great wardrobe of television clothes, which are different. You can sometimes wear them in real life but more often you can't. If I'm going to a smart lunch I might aim for the better taste Joan Collins power suit, but it's not really me.

Sensible dressing isn't me, either. For instance, I would rather die than wear a pair of wellingtons. I would rather go barefoot in the snow or mud than own wellingtons. *Maybe* pink ones could change my mind – then, of course, they wouldn't be sensible.

When I was nine or ten I got very carried away with religion – all that incense and drama. But I was also very worried that when I got older I might want to be a nun. And I thought to myself, 'Please God, don't let me become a nun. Please don't call me – I *can't stand the outfit*.'

I'd seen what I looked like in those bathing hats one wore as a child which made you look like a skinned rabbit. There was my great big moon face sticking out of it. And I thought that's what I'd look like in a wimple. And *no make-up*. I worried about this for some time, until I thought, 'It's okay, if you don't want to do it, you don't want to do it. If He calls, you can always go deaf.'

I *adore* clothes, great outfits are lovely but clothes are not the first thing I notice about anyone – unless they look completely frightful. I suppose it's too obvious to say that Fergie fits that category perfectly? She looks a complete frump, like a cow that's charged through a washing-line. It is difficult if you're bigger but because I understand the problem, I'm less sympathetic.

At the other end of the scale, being totally objective I

can grudgingly admit that Selina Scott looks superb. I just wish she wouldn't try to be more than the perfect clothes-horse she is. The key to her success is that she looks so stunning – or should I say stunned? – as if the base of her skull had been thumped with a sock full of wet sand.

I suppose when one bitches about other women there's got to be an element of jealousy. You could spend your life eating your heart out and wishing you were the girl down the road or your ex-boyfriend's current girlfriend. You could wish your life away moaning, 'If only . . . I wore clothes like that, or looked like that, or was three inches taller, or had a straighter nose, or . . .' But it's a waste of time and I *really* wouldn't want to look like Selina Scott.

I want to look like a better version of me – a thinner, smarter version of me.

You can get Fonda being fit

I would have rather died than admit this till fairly recently but now I can come out of the closet and confess it: despite being one of those women who always sneered at fit people, I secretly envied them. I would have done a body swap with Jane Fonda any day. But the one thing I wasn't prepared to do was put any effort into getting fit myself. If I'd been able to buy her taut, trim torso in the Designer Room at Harrods I'd have bought two, one as a spare. But I thought exercise was disgusting and anything that remotely resembled an athletic garment, I didn't want to know about. I thought it was revolting to sweat and if anyone had asked me where to buy the best sportswear I'd have said Janet Reger. I thought stockings and suspenders were far more sporty than a leotard or, God forbid, a tracksuit.

The trouble with sport at school is that it shapes your outlook on life. If you are not sporty and athletic but always lumbering behind everyone else on the field you become the odd one out, the one who is always last to be picked for a team. If there's an odd number, you are always the one left over which causes a fight between the captains over who doesn't have you. It does nothing to engender team spirit and for that I'm eternally grateful. On the other hand it's hell being one of the unchosen few but on the other hand, once you get into team spirit it is hard to step out of it.

If you're so cosily supported by other people you may never do anything individual. There comes a time when you think, 'Stuff them, I don't want to be in their sodding team – I'd rather compete against myself.' Being the odd one out makes you competitive but in a different way: you don't have to beat other people.

There are two ways of winning and coming out in front. One is straightforward – you do it furthest or fastest or longest. The other way is competing to be best, to do your personal best without much reliance on other people. That's the kind that appeals to me, I discovered late in life – but not too late to do something about it. If only school sport hadn't jaundiced my view of fitness I might have turned into a Green Goddess instead of a Great White Whale.

The most off-putting thing about school sport was the gym knickers, those great navy fleecy-lined bloomers designed to make your bum look like a barrage balloon. And when you're tubby you're always in goal, even if you're as short as me. So there I was, a little round ball of misery with all these huge women thundering down the field at me.

I was also turned off anything athletic by the people who were good at it. Sporty people are not often the sort of people you want to have a conversation with.

The one thing my mother did for me was send me to ballet classes as a child. I think she sent me there because I was such a tubby little thing. In desperation she did that rather than stop feeding me. But I loved dancing and maybe the four years I did it have stood me in good stead because I now have a strong back and have always been relatively supple. I could always touch my toes, however tubby I got. I like to think that when I pass out I do it gracefully, perhaps even with my toes pointed. But I could be wrong.

My first public performance, aged four, was in a dancing school concert where I proved I was no sugar plum fairy – I looked more like an irate pumpkin thumping about the stage. In fact I was meant to be a ladybird – no doubt because of their rotund shape.

So my childhood exercise mostly involved avoiding anything more strenuous than licking an ice-cream. I never climbed trees because I was terrified of heights. In the gym I used to work my way backwards down the queue when they were doing vaulting. As for diving, I was so useless I had to be pushed to go off the top board. I was never what you might call hearty and therefore I was never fit.

I more or less congealed until I was forty. I once did a yoga class – after which I had to come home and have two large vodkas. It is supposed to make you serene but it did no such thing for me. It just screwed me up a bit more.

Then in Guadeloupe on that fateful holiday I was surrounded by people with thin thighs running around being athletic – which was a bit irritating because although I was having a good time, I realised I could have a better time if I was thinner and fitter. I had enormous energy, stamina and willpower but none of it was getting me anywhere.

One morning at breakfast I was incredibly hungover and sat, by chance, next to this wonderfully good-looking French guy who looked like Adam Ant. His name was Stefan and he was the tennis coach.

I said I hadn't played tennis since I was a child and so he asked me to come to his tennis class. He was irresistible – he had to be, to get me stepping out in a pair of trainers. But I did warn him I was hopeless, with no co-ordination, and no eye for the ball. He just said, 'But that's only what one person say to you. You don't know, they may be wrong, it's a long time ago, you come to my class, I teach you in my beginner class.'

Tennis was one sport I always loved to watch and sometimes wished I played. I once played a game in Dundee with Elton John. There was a band playing twenty miles out of town who I went to interview and on stage with them, playing the organ, was Elton sitting in for the regular organist who was ill. In those days he was passionate about tennis so the next day we went to one of the public courts and had a good afternoon bashing a ball around before they left town for their next gig. I got a fearful bollocking when I got back to the office because I shouldn't have taken the afternoon off.

Anyway, I staggered on to the court in Guadeloupe at 8 a.m. the next day and after about ten minutes I was hanging off the back netting like a ripe tomato about to explode, heart thudding and sweat pouring off. I thought I was going to have a seizure, but I actually enjoyed the tennis bit. He was such a good teacher and apart from that, so good-looking and therefore good to watch. He gave me such tremendous confidence that I dragged myself there every morning after that, always with a hangover. And at the end of the week I won the ladies' beginners' tennis tournament. That gave me such a thrill, I couldn't believe it. I didn't immediately rush off and play tennis back home, but six months later, on another holiday, I did the same thing: had a week of lessons and won the beginners' tournament. At that point I realised if I wanted to play tennis I was going to have to be fit – because otherwise I would have a heart attack.

So the second week of that holiday, in Senegal, I started going to the odd exercise class. I found I could stagger through that, so when I came back I went and bought the 'Jane Fonda New Workout Video'.

I lay on the sofa and ate chocolates and watched it for six weeks wondering why I wasn't getting any fitter. In the end I thought I'd have a go. There's a beginners' section which lasts thirty-five minutes, with an eight-minute warm up and about twelve minutes of aerobics. I got about two minutes into the aerobic section and thought I was going to die on the carpet in my front room. I don't know what made me keep on doing it but it might have been the thought that it was my last chance before ossifying and turning to stone. My fat might solidify and I would never move again.

After about a week I began to see an improvement. About two months later I went on another holiday and the difference in the way I felt was amazing. It meant I could stay up drinking and dancing later and get up earlier. I began to see that fitness had something going for it.

I also started having tennis lessons and though I'm not brilliant I can see improvement all the time. I enjoy it as well, which I *never* thought I could. I also do workout classes every day except Sunday.

Even so I'm not the right shape yet. I suppose I'm undoing forty years of fatness and unfitness. I'm trying to reverse the trend.

The hardest part of finding fitness is well behind me but even as a confirmed shopaholic I was almost defeated by shopping for leotards. My first idea was to get something amazing from Pineapple but I couldn't get into anything they stocked. I ended up with a pink and black striped leotard and black footless tights from Harrods which must have made me look like a demented licorice allsort or a wasp on LSD.

The awfulness of taking a size 14 leotard into a changing room is almost indescribable. When you stuff yourself into it you think, 'Well, at least it holds everything together, and stops you wobbling'. Then you turn sideways and your tits are completely flattened, you have to hold your breath to see your waistline. It practically makes you cry.

During the recent London Tube strike I couldn't find a cab and had to walk home in very high heels. As I set off I was complaining in my head about it. Then I thought, 'What are you on about? What do you do those bloody fitness classes for if you can't actually walk? You may not want to walk – but a few years ago you *couldn't* have walked that distance without feeling dreadful.' This time I found it merely boring.

I admit I've always been able to walk from shop to

shop, but a quick totter round Knightsbridge in sling-backs I do not equate with a hearty walk. Although I'm fit, I don't see the point of walking as a means of passing the time or as exercise. (Why people trudge over Hamp-stead Heath, through all that dogshit, I'll never under-stand.)

Inside me there is still an awful lot of sloth. I wouldn't walk round the corner to the shops even though it would do me some good. I'll always get in the car. Why walk? I'd rather save my energy for falling off my stilettos and picking myself up afterwards.

Women are much more sensible about sport than men. I've always wondered why men feel the need to follow teams, to huddle together and bolster each other. It's so pathetic and adolescent, supporting your team and wear-ing its colours. Women don't do that.

They do watch Wimbledon but that's different. It's one-to-one gladiatorial conflict – and bums in white shorts. Women don't support the game as a religion on the fringe of lunacy. I know women are forced to play hockey as a team game but you don't get hockey hooli-gans rampaging through the capital cities of Europe. You don't get lacrosse louts, do you? What is it with men, what herding extinct makes them do that?

Apart from tennis or Olympics on television, I don't see the point of watching sport. I've never been to a football or a rugby match. And golf is just a panacea for menopausal men with a penchant for repellent trousers. When you look at them, they're not fit at all. Even all that bending over they do isn't good viewing, thanks to the awful check trousers. I don't think I've ever seen an attractive golfer.

Golf, for me, embodies everything I think is dreadful: grotty men, crowds of people unattractively dressed, walking for no purpose at all, and it also attracts all the most hideous men in British showbusiness – the Tarbies, Brucies, Kennies, the sort you'd never dream of bonking in a bunker.

I hardly count darts and snooker as sports. They also attract the two least tasty breeds of men. Darts players are the sort of people who, if they stood next to you in the pub, you'd move. You wouldn't just move down the bar, you'd move to another pub. One of them actually has no front teeth: how he ever managed to get that fat with no teeth I can't imagine.

Snooker players all wear those ghastly shiny trousers which make them look like waiters. You'd think a man in tight black trousers with a white shirt and bow tie would look attractive, but all they look like is particularly sleazy waiters. They look like they smell of kitchen fat – though they probably smell of Brut, which isn't much better.

The only sport where men look reasonably attractive is tennis, though I'll make an exception of Boris Becker. (He looks like a large, over-boiled bratwurst. He has that meaty, pinkish quality about him.) But generally, any man with a tan and wearing white is off to a good start – which is why it's such a shame about cricketers. Most British men are off-white and in cricket flannels they just look like unpainted garden gnomes plonked round the edge of the field. The way they always rub their horrid ball up against their groin doesn't appeal to me much, either.

Footballers are so awful they should be kept apart from the rest of the world. They all look in need of gallons of running water, deodorant and hair-straightener. And why are they all called Kevin? Their least appealing feature is their short, stubby legs which are usually bandy and not improved by those hideous long socks. The trouble with sport on television is that it's all aimed at men. If it wasn't, they would make sure footballers had decent hairstyles and not those ghastly style-free Seventies matted ringlets or shapeless Noel Edmonds jobs. David Icke (pronounced Yuck) has a typical footballer's haircut – longish and badly in need of a trim, a bit like my window boxes. In fact, when I think of it, you can always tell a Green by the duff haircut. Vote for split ends and dandruff?

The whole thing about watching men at play is seeing their legs and bums in shorts. But I don't like to see them in less than that. Swimming trunks are not the same thing at all – especially those revolting thong things. There's nothing worse than a man sleazing round the beach in those. But the sight of a really cute, neat bum in white shorts is my idea of a perfect view. Even though I like the fashion for long shorts, they are not very good for bum-watching. Boxer shorts are better. And as for cycling shorts, in action, they could bring me near to hysteria level. With laughter, that is.

No doubt the sight of me in little tennis things covered in Virginia Slims logos is not every man's favourite fantasy, either. But luckily none of my sporting activities is of a standard likely to be seen by millions of TV viewers.

There was only ever one sporting moment when I performed to perfection. And there is never likely to be a repeat. Having been unable to climb trees because I was scared of heights, I found myself a few years ago on a converted German ferry with twenty passengers and eight crew, and the first night at dinner I got rather raucous and promised everyone I would dive off the top rail into the sea before the fortnight's holiday was up. I don't know why I said this, probably just because I was on a boat and felt like being Nautical Nina . . . Because we were swimming off this boat you either had to go down a little ladder or dive over the side and because I'd learned to dive as a child, I could do it. So I practised by diving off the blunt end and off the pointed end and by the end of the fortnight I was feeling reasonably confident. After lunch on the final day I thought, 'I made that stupid vow, I'd better do it. But I'll wait till everybody's having a siesta and go and do it by myself . . .'.

But when I got there, they were all waiting for me.

'Okay, this is the last day – you've got to do it. Why don't you make an event of it and do one dive off the blunt end, one off the pointy end and one off the top rail?'

'The water's so bloody cold I'm going to freeze every time I swim round.'

'We've found a little drink in the cocktail book to warm you up. It's called a Little Devil and we'll give you one for every time you swim round.'

So I did the first dive and they gave me a drink. And then the second. And finally I climbed up on this rail on the top deck and looked down to the water and thought, 'Thirty feet is a bloody long way down – I could break my back.' Then I looked and saw that twenty-eight people were standing waiting for me to do it. I thought, 'It is possible to back out, nobody wants you to break your neck, don't be weedy about it . . .'. Then I looked down and thought, 'Trust your instincts, you can do it from ten feet, the principle's the same, the technique's the same. As long as you don't think about it you'll be okay . . .'.

So I launched myself. Zen diving. It was the most fantastic sensation and I'll never do it again, please God. I actually felt I was going through the air like an arrow. It felt wonderful, I entered the water so cleanly and went down so deep I had a chance to pull up my bikini knickers on the way back to the surface. And when I got there and looked up, they were all holding up signs they'd made saying 6.0 like they do in the Olympics. Even if I'd done a duff dive they'd have given it to me. And when I got out of the water, they had another Little Devil ready – only this time they'd made it pink.

About four months later I got a card from a couple who were on the ship whom I didn't know all that well. Along with a photograph of me doing that dive, with my back straight and my toes pointed.

I keep it to prove that if you really want to do something, you can – as long as you're stupid – or drunk – enough.

Life's a beach

My Plan B for life is that if ever everything gets too boring or too much, if I can't be bothered or don't want to cope any more and subsequently fetch up as a bag lady, I shall flog the flat, pay off the mortgage and go and live in Club Meds around the world till the money runs out.

That may well be a week on Tuesday. But hopefully it will stretch a little further, by which stage I'll speak fluent French, Italian or Spanish and be able to work for my keep, though I don't know in what capacity – probably as resident bag lady. Whatever my role, all I'd want would be to stave off reality for a bit longer.

The whole point of a holiday is that it is *not* reality – it has nothing to do with most people's daily grind. I'd like my reality to be what other people fantasise about – I want to live in a year-round holiday atmosphere. There are ways of achieving a life full of sunshine without being a multi-millionaire or Costa del Criminal so I'm not sure why I haven't become a professional holidaymaker already. But I'm working on it.

I'll never understand the concept of either not taking a holiday or taking a week or two and staying at home. If you can't afford it, that's a shame. But I would rather go without other things, just to travel.

When I was lucky enough to work as a rock writer, it meant lots of travel. That was when I started carrying my passport with me, in my handbag, every single day. Some women carry a toothbrush and a spare pair of knickers but a passport will get you further.

People sometimes say, 'But aren't you afraid of losing it?' No I'm not. And if you carry it all the time, you notice immediately the moment it is missing. You don't have that terrible discovery, half an hour before you're due at the airport, that your passport isn't where you left it. Nor can you simply forget to pack it.

This means I can escape at any time. If somebody irresistible says, 'How about lunch in Paris?' Or dinner in Rome, sailing in St Tropez or carousing in the Caribbean, I can just go. I love the whole escape syndrome, it's my safety valve. I think life should be full of holidays, otherwise it's too much like hard work. Life apart from your job, just organising your day-to-day living, is hard slog – which is why you should make as much of your hols as possible.

I believe in spending as much money as you can spare on holidays because the day you come home you might be run over by a Number 9 bus. If you've got money to spend, a holiday is going to do more for you than new curtains for the living room.

My idea of bliss is tropical sunshine. That may sound obvious – but there *are* puzzling people who choose otherwise. Jungly exotic scenery, exciting new companions, clear turquoise water to swim in, make me a happy girl.

Holidays are one area in which I think I'm well organised – that is, I always go equipped with everything I'm ever going to need. And I am always fully prepared to depart at the drop of a pair of bikini knickers. But that's not to say I get it absolutely right. With me, travelling light means leaving the actual wardrobe behind.

Although you don't wear very much on holiday, you do need lots of clothes with you. I need clothes to go to breakfast in; sunbathing stuff: bikinis and towels and one-pieces; cover-up shirts or big shirts to wear down to

98

the beach – none of your out-dated, sag-bag sarongs, thanks. I need stuff to do exercise classes in, and if I do sport, bras for that. I pack different underwear for when I go out in the evening plus things to change into at lunchtime and clothes for the evening.

As I see it, either you have to take too much to carry – or too little and a credit card. If, like me, you haven't got a credit card, you're stuck with the heavy load.

As soon as I arrive, I know I'm not going to wear half the stuff I've packed. But you've got to take it, just to give yourself a few options. There's no point in having a big suitcase unless you fill it with everything you need to take – and learn to smile about it. You can never have too many bikinis, can you? And whenever you get there you always find someone's got a nicer one than you, anyway. The thing to do with a very heavy suitcase is pretend it's not heavy. You just have to lug it. And watch strong men buckle at the knees as they try to lift it.

The reason people like dressing up at night on holiday is that most of us look a million times better at night – and not just because the light is dimmer. When you're lying round with no make-up and wet hair all day, you look good at night just by contrast.

So – you might have to pack enough to stock Harvey Nichols' leisurewear department but, having arrived in the sun, I think the fewer clothes you wear, the better. The fewer and the smaller. There's nothing worse than seeing a big woman with big bikini knickers. The experts say you should wear one-piece swimsuits with vertical stripes – but they won't make you look thin, you'll just look like a fat woman in a stripey swimsuit. There's nothing that is going to make you look miraculously thinner. The best thing is to get as brown as possible, preferably before take-off. A few sessions on a sunbed well before you go will get rid of that dough-mountain effect. Failing that, an After Sun (with bronzing) will give you a brilliant fake tan *before* – just remember to wash your hands well after applying . . .

One thing you forget when you go to the beach is how boring sand is. I hate sand: it's a really irritating substance. I was going to say it gets up my nose, but that's probably the only place it doesn't get up. People talk about Doing It on the beach but, dear me, the sand falls out of your knickers for days. I suppose the answer is to try doing it on a sunbed.

I once Did It in a Cyprus hotel sauna. Well, it wasn't the original intention. We went there because it was May and cold outside – we were just looking for somewhere to get warm. There was nobody else there so we just locked the door and got down to it. Next time I went back there without him I sent him a postcard from the same hotel saying, sauna and yet so far.

If being cold is miserable on a summer holiday, being over-exposed to blazing heat can spoil your fun just as much. When you've only got seven days or a fortnight in the sun, you don't want to waste time making tanning mistakes, like getting burned on Day One and having to cover up to repair the damage for the rest of the week.

I'm not even considering the question of whether to go topless or not. Surely no one from a country which has Page Three girls would want to go round with the shape of a swimsuit imprinted on their body? You might as well get yourself tattooed like that.

But the problems of toplessness are nothing compared with the pitfalls of going on holiday when you're single. Travelling alone is no problem. It's when you agree to holiday with someone else that you can get into trouble – and I don't mean the sort of trouble that leaves you lying in a darkened room with an ice-pack on your head at the dawn of every new day.

Holiday partners are as hard to pick as Grand National winners. The only way to do it is to decide what you like and what you don't like to do on holiday – then find somebody who enjoys the same things as you. If you don't get this together, you're in big trouble because there's nothing worse than going away with one person or a group of people with whom you are at odds. There's nothing more miserable than being trapped in a tropical paradise with somebody who'd be happier in Hove or with somebody whose leisure interests are entirely different from your own. You then have all the tedium of arranging to meet on the beach before you go waterskiing – and then if you change your mind and don't want to go waterskiing, you still have to go down the beach and tell them. Or maybe you want to go shopping and they don't want to go shopping, so you go shopping anyway and leave them sulking with their book in a bar.

Most single people my age know what they want to do and what they don't. I have an unmarried friend who went out to stay for ten days with her younger, married sister and her husband in a villa in Tuscany. The two sisters had always travelled a lot and always enjoyed the same sort of things but since the younger one got married, she had developed different tastes: she and her husband liked to have stops for coffee and long leisurely lunches in restaurants followed by sightseeing, an ice-cream, some drinks and a potter round the shops and markets.

The older sister liked art galleries. But instead of feasting her eyes on pictures, she spent a whole ten days becoming more and more furious, seething inside and feeling like a spare part. She was with a married couple doing what they wanted and, instead of doing her own thing, she was caving in and going along with them – just because she was a single person. Nobody was forcing anybody to do anything. She should have worked out what she wanted, what she didn't – and got on with it.

I've never been afraid to go away on my own. There are tricks to being on holiday by yourself and as soon as you learn them, you'll have a fabulous time. Rule 1: Go Club Med. Trick One: at the airport and on the plane, start looking at everybody's labels. Then watch them on the way from the airport and try to suss out whether they're people you might want to spend five minutes with. If they're not, it's very easy to avoid them. Trick Two: if they are, make sure you know where they are or make arrangements to meet them at a bar. If all else fails, you can certainly get to know the barman. There will always be someone who speaks English, like the girl who works at the beach. You go and chat to her and meet some people she knows and get to know the gossip.

If you share a room with someone who's a different nationality, you get to meet the people she met on the plane and it snowballs from there. And if you really are stuck, you can always go and join in everything like tennis, waterskiing, gymnastics, windsurfing, go on an excursion, and do whatever is on offer.

In the disco, it's really simple to get to meet people. You just get up and dance and more often than not someone will get up and dance with you. It's a much easier way of mixing and making friends.

Learn a bit of basic language from every country you can think of, as well – especially a few slang expressions or swear words. The language barrier can get very frustrating at times.

I once went on a boat trip where everybody spoke French except for me and the day before we had been to a carpet bazaar so the conversation over dinner was 'tapis' this and 'tapis' that. So I said to the man next to me, who spoke good English, 'I suppose the one good thing about buying a Turkish rug is if you get home and find you don't like it, you can roll it up and smoke it.' He looked blank. I said it was nothing, only a joke. He clapped his hands and announced, 'Nina has made a joke.' I cringed. 'Repeat slowly,' he commanded. I ploughed on carefully and slowly. There was a pause, then one very perplexed man asked, 'But why would you want to smoke an expensive carpet?' I got so frustrated at this point, I rose from the table and jumped overboard in my clothes.

Club Med is nothing like Club 18–30: there are couples, families and all ages. But there are still plenty of singles and opportunities for new friends and holiday flings. The mistake some girls make is in thinking they've found True Love with one of the GOs – the gentils organisateurs, as they call the guys who work for the club, looking after the guests. Any girl who thinks this is going to be the big romance should bear in mind the hundreds of girls the GOs slept with. You should be wary both in terms of safety and your self-respect: you probably think you're special and you probably are, but he will still be looking over your shoulder towards the next lot of arrivals and next week's conquest.

I've seen girls who sleep with guys like that who then think they can't avoid them in the village afterwards. But those guys are brilliant masters of the eye-swerve and know all the ways of getting from A to B without passing the person they don't want to pass. So do not ever imagine it is going to be anything other than a one-nighter.

Europeans understand the concept of holidays better than the British, I think. The British spend far more per head of population on their houses, bunging money into the security of bricks and mortar and not having much left over to *live*. We pour money into our houses rather than on going out three times a week to meet friends in restaurants or cafés, which Europeans do. They are better than us at having fun.

Brits abroad never seem to know how to enjoy themselves. You can always spot them a mile off: they're the ones with the least stylish outfits on the beach, sitting round looking glum. They're strictly to be avoided – always talk fast in any foreign tongue you can manage as you slide away from them. Among the English abroad there doesn't seem to be anything between the Lager Louts and the Hoorays. Except perhaps those middle-class families who are such grey people you could fall asleep looking at them.

Why is it Frenchmen are better at holidays? Why can a Frenchman put on a funny hat and do something silly and it's witty? And when the British do the same kind of thing, it's naff and embarrassing? The French have a lifestyle. But as far as the Brits and style are concerned, style is something you climb over at the edge of a field. But then Brits don't aim to be stylish, do they? We think it's rather bad form.

However I did once meet some holidaying Brits with enough chutzpah, panache and style to make up for the rest. They were in a Club Med (where else?) but they were uninvited guests.

In these holiday villages, there is a funny system of paying with beads for your drinks at the bar. That's about the only thing you need money for. It's a cunning marketing wheeze because you don't know how much they're worth without a lot of complicated calculations. Therefore you don't know what you're spending on each drink. The bead system is also designed to repel invaders: people who come ashore from boats or arrive on the beach can't go to the bar and buy a drink. They can't go and buy beads either because you have to give your room number. However, I can now confess I once aided and abetted a group of invaders.

It was about two in the morning and I was standing in a Club Med nightclub in Turkey when there was a tap on my shoulder and a very Geordie accent said, 'Can you buy us a beer, like?' As I turned round, he said, 'In fact, can you buy us eight beers?' I looked with amazement at the eightsome, all dressed exactly alike, all with a pallor that shrieked New Arrival. They wore orange T-shirts, Dad's Army shorts and great big boots.

'Why on earth should I buy you a beer? You're not Club Med are you?' and their spokesman admitted, 'No, as a matter of fact we're not.'

'How on earth did you get in?' Well, they had come off a big boat that was at anchor in the bay and had come ashore earlier in the day to find nothing much going on. In the distance they spied the Club Med village and asked a local how to get there and were told, 'Don't bother, you can't get in.' This was an irresistible challenge, so they had tunnelled in late at night under the wire perimeter fence and fetched up at the disco. It was like crawling into Colditz.

I thought this was so enterprising I went and got a big bag of beads for them which they found rather puzzling – they didn't quite believe that this would buy the necessary beers.

'The only thing I ask of you is, *don't show me up*.' They were terribly funny and threw themselves onto the floor in a frenzy of breakdancing.

Next morning I dreaded arriving on the beach and finding them still there, sleeping off the night before. But they had gone, vanished, presumably by the same route they had come. I must say I felt quite proud of them.

A part of holidays, I always enjoy, along with stocking up on duty-free scent, is sending back the inevitable postcards. But they *must* be funny – nobody really wants to hear that you're having a good time or how good or bad the weather is. One of the joys of going to Bali was that I could send postcards that just read Bali-Hi! When I went to north Africa I couldn't resist sending back a postcard which read 'As you can see, the Sahara is just a beach.' But then, so is life.

Just an old make-up bag

Beauty Rule Number One is: if you have a spot, you will pick it. No matter what your mother told you, your best friend, *Vogue*, *Harper's*, *Cosmo* or *Woman's Own* told you – though they've *all* told you not to pick your spots, you always will. You will examine every spot in great detail – then you'll pick it. The only person I know who wouldn't is, I suppose, the sort who can open a box of chocolates and only eat *one*. (But she probably wouldn't have spots in the first place.)

So Rule Two is: buy every known lotion, potion, cream, camouflage, everything known to man that is aimed at getting rid of a spot. It won't help but it will pass the time and stop you from feeling depressed as hell while you've got whatever blemish you've got. You'll feel anxious – but you won't feel depressed about it.

The best beauty tip I know is to buy a good pair of sunglasses. I don't mean ones that are good for your eyes, I mean some that cover most of your face. These are an essential piece of equipment, without which you are absolutely stuffed. They cover a multitude of sins, mostly the bags under the eyes. And they shade out the light when you have a hangover from the night before.

After that, people talk about the necessity of a Good Moisturiser and such. I say *rubbish*! Mascara is much more important. Without mascara everybody's face looks like an old boiled potato – or should I say, boiled egg?

After all, potatoes do have eyes. I can't go out without mascara, anywhere. Not unless I want to frighten small children.

Beauty care is a case of making up for disasters. Most beauty experts tell you how to enhance yourself, how to make the most of the good bits. Not enough of them tell you how to cover up the bad ones. If you get really worried, the only thing is to take the sunglasses tip a step further and buy yourself a hat – a bum-concealing hat.

I would recommend spending as much money as possible on whatever products or disguises you can discover. They won't make a damned bit of difference to your spots, bags or wrinkles but at least they'll give you hope. Women like Miriam Stoppard and Esther Rantzen keep saying that you might as well get a vat of vaseline and slap it on your face because it will do as much for you as any expensive cosmetic. But don't tell me that those two women stand there at night and go *Glonk!* with the vaseline. I don't believe it, I bet they buy the whole lot in.

My advice is to buy the pot you like best, the jars you like to look at. Buy as much as you need to spend to make you feel good about it. There is nothing more soothing than spending hours on a routine that may not do you any good but they'll make you feel better. I still stick rigidly to the night and day boring cleansing-toning-moisturising bit.

Not that I don't think moisturising is incredibly important: I started with Elizabeth Arden eye cream when I was eighteen. Nobody told me to do it, so I don't know why I did. But I'm grateful for the result, I'm sure I've got fewer eye bags and wrinkles because of it.

There is nothing more depressing when you sit in front of the mirror than dipping your finger into a pot which you know is the cheapest thing you could buy. Or you squeeze out an economy-size, mega tube of something nasty from a chainstore. I say you should buy every new product that comes out. It'll make the clutter on the dressing table a little bit more attractive, whatever it may do for your face.

The beauty ladies all say things like, 'Set aside one evening for all those little beauty routines like eyebrow-plucking and leg de-fuzzing.' Well, I don't know anyone who has an evening or who wants to do that much work on themselves all at once.

I used to know a girl in the late Sixties who, every Thursday evening, used to cover her entire body with Tanfastic fake tan and on her cheeks she put extra, she shaped her face with Tanfastic. What did she look like? In a word? Orange.

Also every Thursday evening she would iron her hair. People in those days always wanted straight hair but hers was that really, really curly blonde hair, like a big cloud. So she ironed it by laying her hair on the ironing board, putting brown paper over it and pressing it till it was dead straight.

I would go to those lengths, too, for the sake of looking good. For while I don't do domestics around the house, I will take screwdrivers on holiday to do whatever is needed to get the hairdryer or the heated rollers working. I always think I'd be hopeless on a desert island because I wouldn't be able to build anything. But if I put my mind to it, I could get a hairdryer plugged into a palm tree if necessary.

On one holiday in Turkey, the hairdryer plug wouldn't stay in the socket, it had to be wedged with your knee. So a water bottle inside a waste-paper basket, jammed to the wall by a stool on its side, finally did the trick.

Fortunately, I don't have to go to the hairdresser because for years my hair has been cut by my friend Carole, a top freelance stylist who lives near me. I'm thrilled not to have to sit in a salon being patronised by the hairdresser's receptionist – with people like that, you feel obliged to do your hair before you go. Like my mother, who used to clean the house before the cleaner came.

Instead of going to the hairdresser, I go and sit in my friend Carole's kitchen while she cuts my hair. Sometimes I wonder how she can put up with listening to me whingeing while she's doing it. Then I remember that her worst job ever was on a film called *Castaway*, set on an island and filmed in the Seychelles, starring Amanda Donohoe and Oliver Reed. I thought before she went that she'd have a fabulous time out there, and would come back brown and tanned and fit, with not that much hard work because there were only two characters in the whole film.

Well, she came back white and shaking and on the edge of collapse.

'What went wrong, Carole?'

'Every Sunday when it was the crew's day off, I had to work.'

'But why, Carole?'

And she muttered a bit and didn't say much and clearly didn't want to tell me about it – she's very loyal and always keeps secrets. Then she said, 'Well, Amanda was a lovely girl and she was supposed to be blonde and the action is supposed to take place over a year. Naturally her character's hair got blonder in the sunshine, and her hair had to be made varying shades of blonde during the film. But they were shooting out of sequence and there was a lot of going in and out of the water so they couldn't use hairpieces and it was very difficult.'

'Come on, Carole, these are problems you encounter all the time. What *was* the problem?'

Finally she let me have it: she spent every Sunday dyeing Oliver Reed's pubes.

You know how you sometimes lie on a beach pondering such problems as 'Who should I least like to sleep with?' or 'What is the worst thing you could imagine doing?' Well, this was one of those. It's so disgusting you would never begin to imagine it. The guy he played had ginger hair so she had to dye his pubes ginger.

I said, 'How did you do it?' and she said she had to wrap his willie in a plastic bag. So there *are* worse things in life than Nina's split ends.

There have been two things that changed my life. One was getting thinner and the other was going blonde. All my life I had very dark hair and you can say, 'Oh, dark and dramatic' or 'Dark and passionate!' But there is nothing to equate with going blonde. You feel completely different – more frivolous and out for fun. People treat you differently, not your friends but everyone else. It's superficial of course but if beauty is only skin deep, you might as well have what you like.

I remember I was very worried about changing the colour and I had a few very tiny highlights round my face, then I thought, 'Why be hesitant, let's do the lot.' I had it sort of marmalised first, like a marmalade tabby cat. Then I went a bit blonder and then I put crazy colour in and went pink – to match my eyes. I went pink for about nine months and I loved it. It was called Pinkissimo and because it went through highlighted hair, it went all different shades of pink.

I remember standing in Oxford Circus one summer, well after the punk era. As I waited to cross at the lights, an American couple started nudging each other and looking at my hair. Finally the man came over to me and said, 'Excuse me, is that punk hair?'

'No, I'm sorry it's not. In this country we call it pink.'

I hadn't meant to be nasty but fortunately they laughed. Americans can be very bizarre . . .

I have had disastrous haircuts. A guy once cut my hair so short I had to go out and buy a wig. I remember waking up in the night and tugging it and crying. You cry and cry, but there's nothing you can do when your hair is half an inch all over.

I suppose the answer to looking after your hair is to have a much shorter cut but I'm used to fiddling with hair because I'm one of the roller generation, I can jam in the heated rollers like a treat. But I remember when I was at school I used to push plastic rollers into my hair and then had to learn to sleep with my forehead on my hands. When I woke up in the middle of the night my arms

110

would be numb, completely dead from the shoulders down.

The hair on your head may be an endless source of pain and stress but that is nothing compared with the aggravation of dealing with the hair on your body. There used to be a time that when I crossed my legs it was like Velcro meshing.

I've tried everything – those damned creams were the worst, they asphyxiate you with the smell. What I've settled for at the moment is taking my legs every month to Harvey Nichols where a fierce woman waxes them off with hot wax. This is not high on my pleasure graph but at least it's fast. And however brave you are I don't know anybody who would actually say, 'I can't wait – I'm going to get my bikini-line waxed.' That is the pits – embarrassing, and painful.

My friend Frances Edmonds had electrolysis on her bikini line, which took *forever*. But she no longer has to have it waxed, it's gone. When she went into labour with her first baby I spoke to her on the phone and asked, 'Is it painful?' And she said, 'God no, not to those of us who have had electrolysis on our bikini line. Nothing compares with that.'

It's another fact of beauty care that however much you spend on nail varnish it will always chip. And if you apply base coat, nail varnish and top coat, it will all come off in a lump rather than just chipping round the edges. I wish I was the sort of person who could take a long time over their nails, letting each coat dry in between applications. But I always do it just as I'm on the way out of the door. And if you're like me then you must know you have to be completely dressed with your jacket or coat on and whatever you need ready, your handbag over your shoulder and the keys in your hand so that you don't have to pick anything else up. As long as you know that's what you do, it's okay. But I'm never ready in time, I dither round starting things and not finishing them, and I'm constantly late. So I am always doing my nails in the back of a taxi. That's fine until you get to the last two fingers of the right hand. They're the hardest because you have to hold the bottle at just the right angle so you don't spill it. Spills are very much part of my life.

I have to be aware all the time that I'm messy. I just *know* that if I'm putting foundation on, at some moment I am going to put my hand on my white jeans. You learn that you have this potential for doing such things, you know that if you have hands covered in make-up they will be irresistibly attracted to whatever pristine garment you have put on five seconds before.

There is some part of me that wishes I wasn't weedy about hairy armpits and just said, right on, women should be able to have Sherwood Forest beneath their arms and nobody should think twice about it. But I hate the sight of them. And it's funny but it is always girls in those rather traily, Indian-ish, old Monsoon frocks who have the hairiest armpits. It's not butch-looking women in trousers, it's always rather fey women in frocks who also have long, crinkly, Rapunzel-type hair. It always makes me wince.

Of all the hair-removing gadgets you can't beat tweez- ers. I have this nightmare of either losing my tweezers or breaking my right arm. How did Gloria Hunniford tweeze her eyebrows after she broke her arm? That's the first thing I thought when I heard about her tennis acci- dent: poor Gloria, she can't tweeze her eyebrows.

One of the nice things about being made up by artistes for television is you get to learn various tips – like how *not* to make yourself up. It can be a nightmare sometimes because you don't know how it's going to fetch up till it's finished. It's great if you get someone who's done you before and they know what you want but people have their own ideas and it's incredible how they can change the way you look. They can make you look dreadful, not like you at all. You can sit down and ask them to make your eyes as big as possible, try to pretend there are some cheekbones, shade it here, see that I'm quite tanned, these are the colours I'm wearing – and out comes this two-pissholes-in-the-snow effect. You look like an old flour bag, they've spent three-quarters of an hour on your face – and now it's too late to change it. You have to try to repair the damage yourself.

One make-up artist told me if you are prone to greasy skin and have the greasy patches which are the bane of most people's life, so Matte Miracle is the answer (though it sounds more like a character from Thunderbirds or somebody who's in Gary Glitter's backing band). Anyway, you just dot it on your face where it gets greasy and it dries the skin out. There's nothing worse than looking shiny on television or in real life because you look flustered if you're shiny. Otherwise, I've always been very happy about my skin, because as long as it is oily, you're not going to get as wrinkly as people whose skin is like parchment and terribly fragile.

I don't think there is anybody in the world who likes their feet. The best thing you can do about them is learn to accept them, they're never going to look any damned better, they are revolting objects. I'm sure there are people who give themselves pedicures and buff up their soles of their feet and pumice their heels. But I don't. I do go to the chiropodist about once a year to get a corn seen to but as I'm at home a lot, I don't wear shoes much, so I don't have problems.

Feet are frightful but your toes can give you enormous pleasure. Have you ever had your toes sucked? At the beginning you think, 'What's going on here?' But it's wonderful. The other toe treat I'm ecstatic about can only be had if you buy a plane ticket to somewhere hot where the sea is very turquoise blue and clear and there are preferably palm trees. It is then important that your toenails are painted with Christian Dior's Tibet, a very bluey pink which is almost irridescent. You then swim out about twenty feet from the shore and turn over on your back and float and you look past your toenails at the beach and the palm trees and the sky. It's the most wonderful picture – the most fabulous pink against the blue of the sea, with the palm trees against the different blue of the sky. It's my idea of heaven – but without the toenails it is incomplete. If I'm depressed and London's grey and ghastly, I look down at my toenails. And rather than hating my feet, I think of that. My toes cheer me up.

But at the end of the day health is what beauty is all about. They say beauty is only skin deep, a very good reason to look after your skin. Healthwise with me, hypochondria rules. I love going to the doctor. Whatever new pills and potions there are, I have to have them. Most of my holiday packing is pills and potions. I'm obsessive about taking a multi-vitamin pill every day, I also take a zinc and royal jelly capsule every day. In fact, I'll take anything at all that promises to make me better in any way. Perhaps I'm a chemist's groupie rather than a hypochondriac: I don't always think I'm ill but I always have to have every product for every eventuality. It starts with the royal jelly and the multi-vitamins, plus I always keep a pre-menstrual pack of evening primrose oil capsules. Then you need Beecham's Resolve, Alka Seltzer, Nurofen for hangovers, Day Nurse, Night Nurse, antihistamines for allergies, Sudafed decongestant, effervescent vitamin C tablets to ward off colds (I'll take a tube of those in an evening, I overdose on them).

I probably shouldn't say this, but I really like taking pills. It cheers me up to take them: it's a little routine, slamming the pills down. The only thing I've never had to take tablets for is diarrhoea – I've got the constitution of a galvanised bucket. Unfortunately some people say I look like one as well.

No Kidding

I don't think I've ever wanted children – other than other people's reasonably grown-up sons. But I must say the most disconcerting thing happened to me recently when Frances, one of my best friends, had a baby daughter. As somebody who had always shared my views – she didn't like children and always referred to them as ankle-biters – once she had one, she did an about-face and is now completely besotted with it.

So I suppose it must be different when you have your own: people who have their own children can't ever quite understand why you don't love them the same way they do. Not just that you don't love them, you don't like them. Not just that you don't like them, you can't stand them. Left to yourself in a darkened room with them you would probably up-end them in a corner. Or if they were in the line of fire in the supermarket you would run them down with your trolley.

I can't cope with children being cute and made to show off. 'Isn't this adorable? Watch this . . .'. No it's not. It's thrilling for the parents because (I'm trying to be logical and kind to the majority of the population) it's like having a plant or something. Except if something goes wrong, you can't just buy another one from the garden centre. You water it and you watch it flower and put out another leaf or a shoot and that's all fascinating to you. But nobody else gives a monkey's. Why should they? It's nothing to do with them. I think people who become parents should understand this – their children are fascinating to them but to nobody else much at all.

We have a very bad attitude to children in Britain. We neither bring them up in a way where they are treated like human beings or part of the family. Nor are they disciplined enough for them to be regarded as human beings. Who am I to compare? But I've often watched continental children in restaurants abroad. If children are out having dinner with their parents in Italy or France there is no big fuss about them: nobody clucks over them or cuts up their food. They're just there and they just get on with it. With English children there always seems to be a lot of screeching and a big fuss.

I'm all for treating children as children *and* as human beings but as soon as you start treating children as equals, it all falls apart. They are not equals.

It seems to me there are so many unhappy children and unhappy adults who've had dreadful childhoods. How can we allow people to treat children the way we do? It's not just physical abuse but there are children not being loved enough or one child being preferred to another or children being torn apart by divorce or rows. I know childhood can't be all sweetness and light, roses and perfection, and that sometimes you have to face up to the fact that life is not all wonderful. But on the other hand, I don't know how people can put children through it in such a horrible way.

Being single, I've never felt broody about children. In fact I even hate the expression, 'broody'. It conjures up a picture of a chicken wagging its bottom about and getting ready to lay. But I recognise it is a condition that must exist, otherwise people wouldn't have children. I think it's very sad if a woman is single and over forty and suddenly realises she wants children immediately. I knew one woman who was obsessed with the pursuit of children and all I could say to her was, 'Have one'. I can't imagine what sort of parent she would make – probably

116

no worse than anybody else – but she wanted a child to love her in her old age, which seems a terrible reason to have a baby. She was desperate and I said to her, 'Lots of single people have children, why don't you go and do it? It's possible these days.' She had got to the stage where she couldn't look at babies in prams because she thought she was going to steal one. It must be a very sad state to be in.

My fear would be quite the reverse: that I'd have a baby, park it in the pram outside the supermarket and think, 'Take it, someone, take it away'. Then I'd hide round the corner and wait for them to wheel it off.

I don't mind children when you can talk to them but when they're babies and can't tell you what they want or what's wrong with them, they frighten me. I don't know how to handle them. When other people come to show off their new babies, others coo and rush around clucking over them while I have to lock myself in the loo or go out. I don't like to seem churlish but I never know what to do apart from saying, 'Isn't it pretty?' And I never remember babies' names, which immediately tells the parent I'm not interested. If you're interested in the child you do, of course, but not babies of casual acquaintances. I just get terribly embarrassed and say, 'How's the, er, offspring?' or 'How's the small and yowling thing?'

The nicest thing about other people's children is that you can borrow them if you want to – then you can give them back. They're not your responsibility. I couldn't look after a budgie: how could I when I can't even look after myself? I can, just, get together an occasional meal for other people but I could never look after anybody else's general well-being. It's an incredible responsibility and I think if you're irresponsible you should be straight enough to admit it. If somebody said to me, 'Will you look after this child for a day?' I'd be so fraught with the idea, I'd just curl up. This is not to say that children don't like me but I think they sometimes feel they are more grown-up than me. I know friends' daughters always have to inspect me to see what earrings I'm wearing and always expect me to do daft things – they look on me as a curiosity.

The trouble with family life is, even though I know each family's different, there has to be a certain structure to it. And one of the things I like about being single is, although there also has to be a certain structure, you can change it, change the basics and the rules. When you go and stay with a family, you abide by *their* rules. It's lovely to stay with friends at weekends but after forty-eight hours I've had enough. However fond of them I am, whatever age the children are, whether they're tens or eighteens, I think I've become so accustomed to being selfish and having my own space, my own quiet or my own noise, that I just don't want to fit in any more. I don't like compromising. That's selfish, I know. Family life must be compromising all round. The only thing I can think of to recommend it is that I suppose there's always something to do and somebody with whom you can do it.

The most ridiculous thing about not liking children is, I guess, that I never aspired to be a grown-up myself. I don't like grown-ups, I mean the sort of people who were born sixty years old – the bank-manager syndrome. I don't like dull people and I suppose what I'm going through and may never finish is pre-senile adolescence. The whole age thing is bizarre. Although I've never worried about age I do quite like it when people say, 'She's not bad for forty-four.' I've always been totally honest about my years because people find out, so lying seems a waste of time. I like the Joan Collins remark, 'A woman who will tell you her age, will tell you anything,' but it's not true.

I don't always fit in with people my own age, especially married people my own age. I still think that people who are married are older than me. Or people who are taller, are older than me. I once did a television show for Tyne Tees, a discussion programme about whether or not life begins at forty. Everybody in that television studio had been born in 1946, including me and Ken Livingstone. Had we had that birthday yet? Were we nervous, embarrassed, dreading it, lying about it? I looked round that TV studio, and if you looked at it logically, I was clearly in that pre-senile adolescent stage, trying to stave off ageing. I had bright pink hair but it wasn't just that that made me feel I didn't have anything in common with any of them. Some of them looked a generation older than me. Their ideas and way of living had solidified when they got married. They had stopped trying, they hadn't progressed any further. Perhaps it had happened when they had children. Or perhaps a more difficult financial situation brought on by bringing up a family is more wearing. If that's so, it must be dreadful. They were people who looked stacks older than me and I didn't feel I shared anything with them.

My experience of toyboys has shown me that very often I have more in common with the average twenty-year-old than the average forty-year-old. My ideas of fun are still set in that idiotic whirl of loud music, dancing, drinking, clothes, all the frivolous things you like doing when you're twenty. It's just that I haven't changed that much. I have friends in their late forties and friends in their twenties and never the twain should mix. The parents of some friends are only ten years older than some of my other friends. I'm between different generations the whole time which means I always feel either too young or too old. In fact, most of the time I feel perfectly happy being forty-four and being me – but I suspect other people might think I should behave in another way.

If you don't want children, what you have to look out for, if and when you do fall in love, is that that might change your ideas. And while falling in love might be a temporary thing, children are permanent. You can't say, 'Sorry, I've changed my mind. Take it away.'

I've either been very clever or very lucky in that I've never been pregnant. I've never had an abortion but I know plenty of people who have and I certainly would. But I've never had to – so there's luck for you. God knows, I've had dodgy moments, when I've panicked and started jumping up and down and doing lots of strenuous things – even though I know none of that works.

Christmas is a particularly difficult time if you are not with your relations because it's the one time of year when everything is geared to The Family. Whatever the norm is, you deviate from it and feel like a spare part. Even though people are bending over backwards not to let you feel like a stray kitten or a kid lent out by an orphanage, that somehow makes it worse. I don't know any single person who actually enjoys Christmas. They mostly see it as an ordeal, something to be got through.

If you spend it with your family there will always be some awful old aunt who asks, 'So what happened? Why didn't you get married? Why are you on the shelf? And when's your mother going to become a grandmother?'

If you spend it with someone else's family, you go through all their traumas. It's a most stressful time. Everybody fights. There are dreadful family tensions – why put yourself through other people's family tensions when you don't want your own tensions?

You're always so grateful to be invited you turn up with bottles of pink champagne and whole Bries and presents for everybody – and you get given a photograph frame and a packet of bath salts. What's the good of a photograph frame when you haven't got family pictures to put in it?

I think at Christmas you should take yourself off somewhere where there are single people. At least you won't have ankle-biters under foot banging tin drums or breaking all the toys they've just been given. Whatever your idea of Christmas, their idea is something else.

Family festivals are best avoided altogether. But if you're single and feeling miserable on your own, you

No kidding

mustn't blame anybody else. It's down to you. I think you should make your own Christmas, decide what you want to do and just do it. Invite other people if you want to. Or go away somewhere where the natives don't celebrate it.

Knowing New Year's on its way can be depressing as well. You don't want to spend the whole time wishing your head was under the duvet or in the gas oven. For instance, there is a certain time in your life when you have to organise your own birthday parties rather than sulk all day because everyone else has forgotten. Some people don't care about their birthdays, whether they get presents or cards or have parties. (I can't believe that they don't care but they say they don't.) But there comes a time when unless you organise something, there's a chance nobody else will.

So why wait and then be disappointed if nothing happens? You have to do things for yourself if you're single. And you should never allow yourself to feel that being on your own is an undesirable or lonely state. It can be – but being with other people can be twice as horrendous. There's nothing worse than being on your own amongst a crowd of people, like a family. There's nothing lonelier than that. Who wants to be French-kissed by somebody else's whiskery Uncle Harry? And there's always somebody's husband who makes a pass at you in the kitchen as you're trying to stuff the turkey.

Would people still get married if it weren't for kids? I suppose I still think it's nice that if you have kids then you get married. There should be a basis for stability. I'm not saying that if you're single you shouldn't have children. But having had them, it would be nice if you, the parents, could stay together. I have idealistic feelings about marriage. I think marriage vows should be till-death-us-do-part vows, otherwise why make them? Though I know that's not necessarily practical because people change.

But while I wish children happy and stable childhoods,

121

I wish them to happen a million miles from me.

You find children in many places so it's become my policy to go out only at times when children are IN, during school hours preferably and late at night. I never know what to do during long summer evenings when there are kids playing outside – though I suppose I could always make the water bombs from the *Rupert Annual* and retaliate.

I'd never think of going to the zoo in a zillion years and I dread being on a plane trapped near a baby. That could drive me nuts, real teeth-gritting time. I once asked Elton John, 'What about all this business of you wanting children, then?' and he confessed, 'I never really wanted children. You know that. As soon as you sit next to a crying child on a plane you know you don't want one of your own.'

British adults have an irrational attitude towards dogs as well as children. They go 'Aaah' over a dog and there's always much more anger over cruelty to an animal than there is over a child. But while I don't want either, I think I would rather have a dog than a child. They're just as much nuisance as each other but at least a dog doesn't ask 'Why?' every time you say no, it can't have its own way.

My idea of the perfect pet is something totally inanimate – like a stone. But there was something I once fancied in Harrods: a mechanical cat, a great big fluffy thing for about a hundred quid. It was like one of those aeroplanes you track with a bleeper and you could programme it to run around your house. I'd love one of those: you wouldn't have to clean up after it, you wouldn't have to bring it in at night and you wouldn't have to feed it.

I know I'm not very attractive when I express my views on dogs and babies and I could make myself sound loveable by saying, 'Yes, I'd love a dog or I'd love a baby.' *But I wouldn't*. So why pretend?

Films have a lot to answer for in the way they present family life, as in the idealised cute kid in *Kramer vs*

Kramer. The first view you had of it, as it toddled down a little corridor to the loo, you knew you were doomed to a whole filmsworth of cuteness.

Then there was *Fatal Attraction*, that movie where Glenn Close played a woman who had an affair with a married man, played by Michael Douglas. In one scene she follows him home and as he greets the wife and child she is out there in the dark looking through the picture window. She sees him with his family, all lovely and romantic and idealised, kissing the kid – and she threw up in the shrubbery. Well, I was throwing up too, as I watched – not because I was in love with Michael Douglas but because I thought it showed exactly what I don't want in family life.

I have, however, found an infallible way of making children disappear. And it doesn't involve either violence or witchcraft. If some child is being particularly annoying and you can't hit him or kick him because the parents might object, here's what you do.

Just say, 'Come here. I'm going to kiss you.'

A Taurean in a china shop

When Russell Grant first bounced on to our television screens like a beach ball in a jumper, I thought he was terribly camp and very funny – about the only reason for switching on 'Breakfast Time' just after it was launched. So I wrote a couple of lines saying what a relief he was from the dreariness of Selina Scott and Frank Bough.

To my surprise, Russell rang me up and said he wanted to thank me for what I had written.

'But I only wrote a line or two.'

'Yes, but when I think about what you could have written . . . .'.

They were clearly all feeling a bit bruised after a general battering from the critics. He said, 'I don't usually do this, but we've been given such a rough ride.'

He was very funny and we got on well, so well that he offered to do my astrological chart. So about six weeks later I went to his little house in Wembley and he cooked me lunch. I always remember that we were having something with mashed potatoes and he got out this pound pack of butter and took about a third off it – and then dumped the two-thirds into the mashed potato. I thought, 'I love him! Here's someone with a bigger problem than me.'

My star sign is Taurus and when you read what Taureans are supposed to be like, you could be forgiven for thinking they are the least attractive people of the zodiac.

Would you like to be described as plodding and materialistic? As solid, earthy and suffering problems with
weight (they always say that and in my case they're
always bloody right). We Taurean charmers are also said
to be stubborn – which is certainly true of me. I suppose
you could say our lack of grace is that of a Taurean in a
china shop.

When Russell did my chart, he was unnervingly accurate about certain things in my past and he didn't pussy-
foot around in telling me where my troubles lay. Most
people say to you, 'You might have a tendency towards . . .' or 'This could be a problem if you allow
it . . .' or 'There's a hint of something here.' He just
looked at me and said, 'Darling, you're a fucking disaster
with money, aren't you? And you're disastrous in your
relationships.'

I asked what made him say that and he told me. 'Your
Sun in Taurus is what makes you solid, dependable,
materialistic, home-loving and nest-making.' (I'd dispute
the nest-making but the rest is probably right.) He also
told me, 'You are possessive with a need to settle down.
But your Moon is in Sagittarius, the sign of the traveller,
which means you like travelling. I bet every time you see
a plane in the sky you want to be on it.' He was absolutely
right – even if it's only landing at Heathrow, I want to be
on it.

He said that these two signs were pulling against each
other so that if I ever meet someone who wants to settle
down, I will destroy the relationship deliberately. 'You
can't bear to have roots', he said. 'But at the same time
you long to have roots. Therefore you will always fall for
somebody you *know* will never settle down.' So far, that
has always been true.

But he did predict that one day I would strike a balance
between the two and it would all work out. So if you're a
gorgeous twenty-two-year-old with serious nesting instincts, watch out.

One thing he said to me then, in 1983, was that he saw

television in my chart to which I said, 'Very good, Russell, I'm a television critic as you know.' But he said, 'No, I mean television appearances.' He was definitely right there.

I'm not a zodiac maniac but like most people, I suppose, I've always *sort of* believed in astrology. When I started reading Patric Walker in *Nova* magazine in the Sixties, I found him so uncannily, depressingly accurate that I still read him all the time – and still think he's brilliant.

I suppose you read your signs in inverse proportion to whether you are happy with your life or the state of your closest relationship. I find I start reading my stars like crazy if I am worried about a relationship or my career or moving house or something like that. I start reading things into it and reading the other person's star sign. It becomes almost a religion. But in a way I feel you bend astrology to suit your own ends.

I think Russell Grant is fairly psychic though he doesn't claim to be because he says people think you're nuts. But a while ago he rang me up out of the blue one Monday morning when I hadn't spoken to him for several months and said, 'How are you?' And when I said, 'Fine,' he said, 'No, I mean how are you *really*?'

I was forced to tell the bitter truth. 'It's all a bit of a disaster actually.' I'd been freelance for a year and done very little work and decided I didn't want to write any more and signed with a new agent who hadn't got me a single job. I'd put on two stone and felt I was unemployable. It was all *dreadful* and I didn't know how I was going to cope.

'That's what I was worrying about. I woke up this morning very early and I was worrying about you and money. Don't worry, it will come right. Something will happen and you won't at first see that it's a positive thing. But it'll make things happen.'

It was about three weeks later that I was turned over by the *News of the World*. It was fairly awful – but it did shake up my whole life. Work started coming in as a result: I was then asked to take part in discussion programmes about invasion of privacy which was then becoming a hot issue. My whole career started properly from that moment. I started making money, it made me lose weight – and Russell had seen it all about to happen.

Russell has told me I am psychic. So did Doris Collins when I interviewed her on Sky television. I asked her afterwards, 'What on earth do you mean?' And she said, 'You know you're perceptive, you couldn't have been a journalist or interviewed people unless you sensed how they were.'

'That's just intuition.'

'That's halfway to being psychic, it's all part of it.'

Don't worry, though. There's no way I'm setting up a stall, slipping into a gypsy skirt and hoop earrings and telling people that the false teeth are in the grandfather clock.

As far as men go, my ideal partner is supposed to be in my opposite sign of Scorpio. Oddly enough I've never been out with one – apart from the millionaire who dumped me at the ball. He was a Scorpio: that's how I knew when he left that there'd be no going back.

I'm very loyal and I'd do anything for a friend. You can push me quite a long way before I have rows with people, a lot further than most people I know. But once I snap, the drawbridge is up and it doesn't ever come back down. I don't ever forget, I can forgive something horrendous but I can never forget it. I can cut people out of my life quite ruthlessly. But it takes a long time to do that. I discussed it with my millionaire friend once and he said, 'I'm the same. Only Scorpios are faster to do it, they don't give you a second chance.'

I'm not proud of this: I've cut people out and felt no guilt about it. Then I've felt no guilt about feeling no guilt about it. It's very bad – but it's all caught up in the feeling that life's too short.

I suppose we're all superstitious in some way or other. If I'm really wishing for something, I do stupid childish things like telling myself, 'If I get through this next traffic light before it turns red, then what I want *will* happen.' Which is daft because all it means is you put your foot down and roar recklessly through the intersection.

I suppose my biggest superstition is my pink one. When I was doing the 'Derek Jameson Show', I took my own pink mug in every day to make me feel better about the famously revolting BBC coffee. After the first day I did the show, there was a huge bouquet of pink carnations and a bouquet of pink roses from a man friend with a note saying, 'You were rubbish on the radio.' It was, I hope, a joke. So to make myself feel better I'd take in one of the pink roses every day to the studio and put it in a little pink carafe, and I'd have my pink pad and my own pens (I have to have my fine black pen) – and felt comfortable surrounded by all my own things.

When I returned for a second time on the show, I felt I had to continue my pink routine just for good luck. But I'd split up with the man who sent the roses so there were no pink flowers this time. But I thought, 'I *have* to have pink roses on my desk'. Fortunately there is a rose bush in the garden of the people next door, so I nicked one every day for the two weeks (sorry neighbours – did you guess it was me?).

There was one morning when I left my pink briefcase at home with my pink pad in it. By the time I got to the studio it was too late to go back. I tried not to panic about it but when I asked the producer for some paper to write on, he could see I was agitated. And he knew why. So he searched the building and found a block of white paper. Then he found a pink highlighting pen with which he drew a border round the page and wrote on it, 'This is a pink pad'. That made me feel all right again. What a wonderful man and thank you, Brian. I know I'd have been twitchy if he hadn't done it.

My pink thing is a ludicrous obsession, I know. I get depressed if I don't have enough pink around me. I just dwindle. If I was completely removed from pink, people would have to come rushing at me with loads of my favourite colour because it wouldn't be me any more without pink.

The only thing that distresses me about my pink fixation is that Barbara Cartland has it too. I really worry about what we have in common, will I end up like Barbara? I hope not. I hope to die before I get embarrassing – but then I suppose I should have been dead years ago. Perhaps the terrible thing about people who like pink is they don't care about being a joke? Do you think she realises?

What gets up my nose

People often say to me 'How do you feel knowing that people hate you?' Being Nasty Nina, the Bitch on the Box or whatever else they like to call me, attracts more aggro than a Millwall away match. Not everybody loves a critic, it seems.

I have to be honest and admit that it's nice if people like you. But if you don't know them or who they are; you don't respect them or you know nothing about them; how can you care about what they think about you? I don't see that that should be a worry to anybody. I never understood when people used to rail at me for things I'd written. I used to say, 'I don't know what you're worried about, it's only one person's opinion. If you think I'm such an idiot, you must discount what I think.'

I wouldn't dream of going up to someone at a party and telling them their frock would look better as a loose cover on a chair. But someone who is trying to make a career on television is different. It's not radio: part of the job is how people look, it's a very visual, image-conscious age we live in. It's part of the deal. It's no good being like Jim Bowen and saying 'Oh, I think they're smashing. They'll always work.' They certainly won't if they look ridiculous.

I don't think I'd be rude to people for no reason. Though if I got pissed enough . . . maybe . . .

I will, however, *always* have a go at someone who

bumps me in a shop or at a party, without apologising. 'Could you try that again and see if you can really knock me over next time? Let's have one more go at it. Come on. I'll give you a count of ten.' I'll get really bloody-minded about it.

One person's rudeness is another person's honesty. It's all in the mind of the beholder. I went into a tapas bar with friends one night after a gruelling week and there was a middle-aged woman sitting at the bar, obviously a regular. She tottered over to our table, asked to borrow a pen and then having done that started muscling in on the conversation. I thought, 'When I'm pissed I hope I'm not as boring as that.' It was quite late and I was tired but I was having a nice time. This woman was in danger of spoiling it so I decided she had to go. I just looked at her and said, 'If I give you another pen, will you go away for good?'

'Oh, that is so rude!' she said.

'I'm terribly sorry,' I said as politely as I could, 'But you have pushed into our conversation, this is my evening and I want to spend it with my friends. We haven't invited you to sit down and I don't really want to talk to you any more. Would you please go away?'

She said, 'That's so rude.' I replied, 'I'm sorry, life's too short to suffer in silence.' I know it was brutal and selfish of me. But her behaviour was selfish of her.

I don't think you should intrude on other people like that. I'm very aware of space, my own privacy and other people's. And I will always leap to defend it.

There was a famous night at the Groucho Club where I'd gone for a late dinner with friends after the royal premiere of *The Last Emperor*. It was a really long film without an interval, not a choc ice, not a drink so we finally fell into Groucho's where, next to us at the table were a group of Hooray estate agents who had obviously been there all week and had bottles and bottles of drink on their table. They could see we were in a hurry for a drink and while we were waiting to order, they asked if we'd like one of their bottles of white wine. That's why we couldn't complain about their behaviour later.

In fact they were all perfectly all right – except for the one sitting immediately behind me. He kept turning round and prodding me and saying, 'So what's your name, then?' I kept ignoring him till eventually I thought it might shut him up if I told him. 'Oh, never heard of you,' he said. He was a real clever clogs. He was at the stage where he was nearly falling into his wine, so I just kept telling myself, 'Let it go, he'll get sick of it soon, he'll go away.'

Then in walked Eric Clapton with a woman and they sat down at a table for two against the wall. Where upon this fellow behind me went into a catatonic frenzy, craning his neck and muttering, 'Eric Clapton, I'm going to go and talk to him.'

He started to get up, so I turned round and said 'No, don't do that. Leave the man alone. He's come to the club for a quiet dinner.' It had no effect at all. He was raving, 'But I'm a fan of his.'

'I don't care what you are,' I said. 'He owes you nothing. If you want to be a fan of his, that's what you are. I'm sure he's very grateful and all that but he's not somebody who talks, he's somebody who plays the guitar, for God's sake. And he's not here to play the guitar, he's here to have a quiet dinner. Leave the man alone.'

The guy was determined. 'I'm just going to get his autograph,' he said, trying to rise.

At this moment I had my fork in my hand. So I waved it at him and said, 'Right – one more word out of you and it's fork in the bollocks time, orright?'

He went absolutely white and didn't say another word all evening. All the other guys fell about with laughter – and Eric Clapton was left to himself.

A lot of the cross exchanges I have are over bad service, for which Britain is famous. We equate service with

132

servility, it's a class thing. Instead of seeing something as a job to be done, we feel that providing service is in some way demeaning. I say if you're a waitress, be a good waitress, and be happy about it.

I have fights with British Telecom operators over alarm calls. You can only book them on a quarter-hour in London. If I want a call at seven minutes past or twelve minutes past they don't do them. But why then is it that the call comes at seven minutes past? And how come you can wait half an hour at night for someone to answer if you dial 100?

I had a stand-up fight with a BT operator once, over an alarm call for ten o'clock on a Sunday morning. I was awake at five past ten and hadn't had the call, so I rang to say don't bother. They agreed not to charge me. Next thing the phone rang and it was the supervisor who told me, 'Just as you were ringing to complain, we were ringing with your alarm call.'

'Be that as it may, I didn't get it at ten o'clock.'

'But you *would* have had it at ten o'clock.'

'No – because I waited till five past to ring.'

'It's not five past yet.'

So I looked at my watch, at the clock on the wall, at the video – all said it was seven minutes past the hour. She said, 'Look here, dear . . .' and that was it. Anyone who calls me 'dear' is waving a red rag at a bull. 'All I wanted from you was an assurance that you wouldn't charge me for the call. And hopefully an apology for the non-arrival of the service I asked for. But in lieu of that, as I can see there's none coming, I'm going to hang up because there's nothing more I want to say to you.' I was shaking with rage and put the phone down.

On my other line I dialled the speaking clock and by this time it was eight and a half minutes past. So I was right and this woman was wrong. And she'd said, 'Now look here, dear.'

So I dialled 100 again and asked for the supervisor, who by this time was dead snotty. 'Now what time do you say it is?' I demanded. She said it was six minutes past ten. I said: 'Rubbish. You're going by the clock on wall? You're in the business of giving alarm calls? For which you charge people over a pound? Right: will you get the speaking clock on the line so we can both hear it.'

It came through loud and clear: 'At the third stroke it will be 10.10 precisely.'

'Well what do you want me to do about it?'

'Well I had hoped for an apology but I suppose an assurance that you might get the clock fixed would suffice.'

You know what she did? She screamed down the line.'

'What do you think I am, a bloody clock mender?'

'That's going to look great in print isn't it?'

'What do you mean?'

'I think the world should know about this, I think it's outrageous, your behaviour: you've screamed at me, you're in the wrong, and you haven't apologised. Will you give me your name please?'

So she screamed it down the line, middle name and all, and slammed the phone down. It did give me a certain amount of satisfaction.

Another sort of incompetence that really gets me going is the sort I experienced having dinner on TV expenses on a train to Leeds. The waiter came up to me, one of those cheeky, cheery chappies who thinks 'e's a bit of a card. ('I don't live like this and I know you don't eat posh like this, so we're just pretending, like.') He doesn't actually say it but that's his attitude.

'So what would you like?'

'I'll have a Campari and soda.'

'No, no, to eat.'

'I'd like the Campari before I decide, thank you.'

'Oh, the girl will come round.'

When the girl came, I said 'I'll have a Campari and soda and a half bottle of Muscadet.'

The place was full of businessmen all of whom had ordered gin and tonics, including the guy I was travelling with, who had also ordered a half bottle of red wine. When the girl brought him the wine, she asked 'Would you like to try it, sir?'

And he said 'No thank you, I'm sure it will be lovely.'

So she turned to me, plonked down the Campari and soda, plonked down the half bottle of white wine and turned to go.

I got rattled at this point because a) she hadn't asked me to taste it and b) it was white wine, it was going to get warm – supposing it had been cold in the first place. So I said to her, 'Excuse me, could you take the white wine away please?' A complete blank stare. I asked, 'Would you mind taking the white wine away and putting it in an ice bucket or wherever you got it from so it will keep cool?' Then she said something I've only ever heard said in sitcoms before, 'Yer wha?'

So I said it again, 'Could you take the wine away, please?'

'Yer want me ter take it away?'

'Yes please.'

'Yer want me to take it *away*?'

'Yes please, I'd like it chilled to drink when my dinner comes.'

'Shall I not leave it, then?'

'No. *Will you take it away?*' I wanted to add 'And shove it up your arse. It's probably colder there.' But I restrained myself and just said, 'Take. it. away. and. put. it. in. the. fridge.'

All the men were cowering as they waited for their soup – you could tell by their ties that they aways had soup. I sat there and looked out of the window as I drank my Campari.

Next thing, back came the cheeky chappie with a row of plates up his arm, saying 'Oo's fer the salad, 'oo's fer the salad.' And with a great swoop he tried to put it down in front of me.

'Are you not salmon salad?'

'Yes, but not yet.'

'Is there a problem then?' he asked with the hint of a sneer.

Then I'm afraid I turned into Lady Bracknell – that's what British Rail does to me – and said down my nose, 'I had *hoped* I'd have the grapefruit cocktail first.'

'Oh,' he said. 'Aven't you 'ad it then?'

'No, I'm enjoying my Campari but that's all I've had so far.'

It was like a farce from then on. The grapefruit came but then the salmon didn't. And I had to ask four times for the wine. They then charged nearly twenty quid. What *do* you do about that? All right I'm lucky to be having dinner on a train – but why do we Brits put up with crap?

I'm always the one who just opens my mouth and puts my foot in it. I'm always the loudmouth who says, 'But – you promised.' Or 'This isn't right.' Or 'You said . . .' Or 'This isn't what's in the brochure.'

Top of my rudeness chart are middle-aged men. Menopausal men, whatever race they are, seem to be excessively bad-mannered and pushy. They also seem to hate strong women. I find my greatest enemies in show business have been middle-aged men like Jimmy Tarbuck (I'd include Max Bygraves but he's too old) and even Alan Coren, a wonderful writer but clearly unable to deal with women like me.

On Radio Four's 'The News Quiz', I was once in Richard Ingrams' team – a rare and lovely older man, he reminds me of an unravelling cardigan. When I said to him, 'I don't want to let you down,' he said 'No, no, don't worry. My team never wins, it's my thing. I don't care about winning – but watch Coren, he gets like a turkey if he isn't winning, he really gets excited.'

Now I had done my homework and I knew the answers, certainly all of ours, so I'd write them down for Richard. And as we were winning, Coren seemed to me to get redder and redder in the face and started talking over me.

Next time I did the show, I was terrified. I was on his team and I didn't let him down either. However, he obviously doesn't care for me because shortly after that he cut me dead at a party.

I find middle-aged men terribly crabby. Like Max Bygraves, who refused to go in the same box as me for a final of 'New Faces'. He expected, perhaps, that they would throw me off the show. They threw him out instead. It took him about eight hours to come up with a quote reacting to it: 'Sharing a box with her would be like sharing the back seat of a Volkswagen with Adolf Hitler – except with Hitler there would have been more room because he was thinner.'

When I was asked for my response I said, 'At the risk of sounding pompous, it is my job as a panellist on "New Faces" to make remarks about talent. Therefore, I have nothing to say about Max Bygraves.'

On the show, the first act was a singer called Max Bacon. I couldn't resist saying, 'Thank God it's the only Singalonga Max tonight', and the whole audience went, 'Yeeeaaah.' It was wonderful. I hope he choked at home.

Stars can be inexcusably rude. I once went to Germany to interview Shakin Stevens, which was a big deal then because he hadn't been interviewed for a long time. They were terrified that it would come out that he was married with three kids and not the wonderful single Adonis that everyone thought he wasn't.

His manager was a kind of woman-mountain who was to him what the Colonel was to Elvis and after a couple of glasses of wine we went down from the suite to an incredibly grand lunch. Shaky and I sat at one end of the table and the manager was at the other with someone from the record company. So I got on with the interview, which was hard going. You've heard about the man who was so thick he sported splinters rather than dandruff?

When I asked Shaky if his movements were choreographed for him he got very twitchy and said, 'No, no, no. All my own movements.' Then I asked, 'How do you keep in shape? Do you work out?' And he said, 'No, no, no – it's just natural!'

'Gosh, you don't go to dance class or anything?'

'No, no, no.'

'That's wonderful,' I said admiringly. 'Do you like dancing? You must do it a lot – do you shake at parties and that sort of thing?'

'How dare you!'

I was puzzled. 'What? What do you mean?'

'How dare you ask me questions about my sex life?'

Dumbstruck, I apologised, 'I'm sorry, I was simply asking if you enjoyed dancing at parties because a lot of people who enjoy performing on stage are very shy when it comes to social gatherings. But if you're a natural mover . . .'

'You don't fool me,' he snarled. 'I know you were trying to ask me about my sex life. You think you're very clever you journalists but I've got the better of you. Here's what I think about you journalists . . . .'

And he put two fingers in the air and continued the movement till the fingers went straight up my nose, up these very nostrils. In the middle of this extremely exquisite, very elegant, extraordinarily expensive restaurant.

What does one do then? It's not something the etiquette books tell you. Happily, Shaky removed his fingers, watched by his manager who was looking aghast at the other end of the table. He didn't apologise. I simply said 'I can't quite believe that's happened.' However, the interview continued and when I wrote it up, I included the incident.

I thought it was pretty unacceptable behaviour and I was even more staggered when the manager rang up and tried to pretend that what I'd written hadn't happened.

A different sort of male behaviour which gets up my nose is when someone starts to kiss you and immediately sticks his tongue down your throat. It's disgusting. It's such a shock to the system. It's like someone taking you out to dinner and shoving a whole Big Mac in your mouth.

'Would you like some dinner?' 'Okay.' SPLODGE.

I once went out with an absolutely beautiful Italian, about six-foot-two, dark-haired, a PhD, spoke with a wonderful accent, everything a woman could lust after. He was wearing butter-soft leather boots, wonderful jacket, wonderful trousers. I was introduced to him at Stringfellows and we roared back to my place. We didn't even maka da coffee, nothing like that. Everything was going wonderfully well when suddenly he shouted, 'Hava my bambino.' It was like having a bucket of cold water poured over you. I leaped straight in the air off the bed and shouted, 'If you want a bambino, go down to Mothercare.'

I was reminded of him afterwards when I had to test an Italian espresso coffee machine for a magazine. It was sleek, stylish, expensive to maintain, with a disconcerting tendency to be drippy. I decided the machine was preferable to the man – better a constant drip than an inconstant drip.

Some women, of course, may not mind the Italian stallion approach to sex. Presumably they'd rather be asked to make babies than simply enjoy the exercise most succinctly described by one old-fashioned four-letter word.

Bad language is obviously offensive to a lot of people – but I've never been able to understand what is so obnoxious about swearing. People write letters to the paper about it, they ring up radio stations if you say 'Damn'. I said 'knackered' on Radio Two once and I got chastised for it. I asked the producer, 'What's wrong with "knackered"?' and he told me, 'On Radio Two, knackered is more of an *evening* word.'

I was tempted to say 'You should fuckin' 'ear what I do say in the evening – you'd be stark bollock naked amazed.'

I know my language is terrible: I blame it all on my rock 'n' roll days. I say 'Oh God' all the time, which I know is blaspheming, but we don't care about religion in Britain, do we? And anyway, I like swearing, I really do. You can make it really funny. There are so many ways you can say 'Fuck off.'

A few years ago, 'bugger' was never heard on television and you never heard 'pissed' – though you saw it a lot.

There are things people say to each other that I find far more offensive than swearing. About the worst thing you can say to someone, I think, is, 'You need a holiday.' It's just another way of saying, 'You look like shit and you're behaving like an arse-hole.'

Some people say very unthinking, unkind things. Like, 'I love your hair like that. It looks so much better.' Better than what? What did I look like before? Godzilla?

The worst things men say to you, especially men you've never met are things like, 'Cheer up love, it may never happen.' And you say, 'Yes it did, you just spoke to me.' Or, 'Come on darling, give us a smile.' The only answer to that is *FUCK OFF*. There are other answers but that's the only effective one.

Those male lines imply that women are only there to smile at them and look pretty and give them pleasure. You can, of course, always give them the old Italian one-finger sign.

The incredible shrinking woman

I'd hate anyone to think this book was saying, 'Look at me, aren't I wonderful? Isn't my life perfect? Look how I've lost weight! Isn't it fantastic!' I'm afraid it isn't. I'm still the woman who buys a £54 pair of fuschia buckskin shoes in Harrods sale for £20 – then sticks one foot in a cup of coffee the first time I wear them.

Take this book. Even though I'm sometimes called a journalist I haven't actually written a word, I've just talked a lot. I like to imagine I get away with things but it doesn't actually work like that. After we decided that the way to do it was for me to talk into a tape recorder and Ros to write, I said, 'There's no point in sitting talking in London, why don't we go and sit on a beach and talk?' So I organised a Club Med holiday in Turkey for us: work the first week, have a holiday the second. And everyone said, 'Lucky bitch.'

It sounded a smooth scenario but you know me by now – the actual work got done but the pleasure bit was a very near-disaster. Just before we went I had my legs waxed and on the first morning on the beach I looked at my legs and couldn't believe it – they were covered with what I can only describe as pustules. Disgusting. About sixty on each leg. They made me feel so bloody attractive I used to pray for darkness each day. After a week I went to the nurse and I thought she'd say, 'Well, it's an infection, it's very common here in Turkey due to cheap suntan oil' or

141

some such explanation. But no. what they said was, 'C'est bizarre' and 'C'est incroyable' and 'Qu'est-ce que c'est?' and they kept calling people to look at my legs. On top of that, as the legs began to clear, I got felled by a horrendous virus. It's the only holiday I ever hated.

So even though people said, 'Lucky cow, she's swanned off to write a book she's not writing,' it was yet another Nina nightmare. So please don't think I'm saying, 'Look at me, aren't I great?' because I'm not.

My life is a total fuck-up. It's simply that if your life is lived butter side down, you must try to view it sunnyside up. It's a question of making the best of the bad bits.

In the light of this lifetime of disasters, I have to ask myself, 'What have I learned?' Apart of course from the fact that there is only one useful effective thing to teach a man sexually: to take his socks off *before* his trousers.

Well, running through it all, you can see the obsession with weight, the dieting and eating – but even though it took forty years, I have learned that I can actually control it to a great extent. I've now kept two and a half stones off for eighteen months, the longest ever time I've been an easy size twelve.

I've done it by stepping up my exercise regime so that sometimes I can go off the rails: on a balmy holiday in Bali I lived on fish and vegetables – but at night I drank like a fish. There, too, I ate everything at Christmas and New Year and everything on the plane home (for thirty hours what else is there to do?), arrived home drunk and constipated – and hadn't put on an ounce.

I go to at least one exercise class a day and push myself hard. I can do the high impact body blitz aerobics for a minimum of an hour, I do body conditioning, I do low impact fat burners. That has become my religion, the focus of my life in a way. And it works. I think for the first time in my life I've got my metabolism right. It's taken three years and at last I seem to have struck a balance. I can walk across a beach without thinking about it, without holding my stomach in and trying not to wobble. It's such a joy. I can eat pudding when I go out to dinner – whereas before I used to refuse it, then go home and eat.

It's the old formula they always tell you works: diet and exercise. And you just don't believe it. It takes forever – three years so far – but you've got to do it before it's too late. (I sometimes think that if I was doing a degree in something for my brain, it would take me three years to do that. Well, I've started off with a primary school body and I'm up to O-level standard. I started with a completely illiterate body and changed it into something that's passed a few exams. It's not brilliant yet but I'll get there one day.)

There are women around who try to tell you it's all right to be fat. That may be so – but not for me. I think letting yourself be fat and wearing drab tents and support sandals is a negation of sexuality, it's somebody who's not prepared to take life and sex and accept it and be part of it. It's nothing to do with being hungry or greedy or liking chocolate, it's somebody who is scared of living. It's also a defence against middle-class pushy parents who want you to achieve, it's a defence against growing up and being part of life. Women like that use their fat as a barrier against life. They think: if I was thin, everything would be okay. But once you've lost weight you still have to face up to your problems and life – and you still haven't got the safety net, the excuse of fatness.

Besides – I fancy men who fancy thinner women, I don't fancy men who fancy elephantine sixteen-stone women who look like their grannies. So what is the point of looking like that?

Okay, I've got my weight in order these days but, as they say in the tabloids, that's not all, folks. Getting your life in order is another matter. And here the big point to make is that everything I've managed to do is thanks to someone else. When you live on your own there are certain people who take on greater significance in your life. You need men (obvious) but ones like my wonderful

143

accountant, wonderful lawyer, a hairdresser, a number of people who've helped me to lose weight, friends like the girl who waxes my legs, another who does my corn – and every other kind of friend who's been supportive. Friendship is the most important thing.

My friend Frances Edmonds, for instance, absolutely understands the need for going out and getting blitzed because she's a hooligan too. We've done wonderful, dreadful things – the last time I went to her place I ended up falling headfirst into the grand piano at four o'clock in the morning. You need support from friends like that, apart from anything else it's reassuring to know that there's someone else who can behave as badly as you.

Then there are friends who'll listen while you whinge on endlessly about what he said to you and what you said to him. And other people who do your nails, and girls in favourite shops who'll be honest with you when you try something on and will say, 'No, it's not you.'

Then, above all, there's the person who got me to the state I am today, this cheerful mess that I am – my shrink Dr H.

People often don't admit to seeing a psychiatrist for fear of everyone saying, 'She must be nuts'. I know a lot of people who go to shrinks but never talk about it, because they're ashamed of it and think it's a very unBritish thing to do. Going to shrinks seems to them to be a very American, arrogant, self-indulgent thing, something you do if you've got too much money and self-importance.

I disagree. I first went to a shrink a decade ago because I cracked up, I actually ground to a halt physically and mentally. The way I was living was a total disaster, I was travelling round the world as a journalist, achieving a lot, but I couldn't get my mental state right. It was a nightmare of lost sleep and night after night lying awake at my wits' end, not knowing what to do or what I wanted.

I stopped being able to make decisions and any little setback had me bursting into tears. Eventually I was driving to the office, crying all the way there, going out to interview someone, crying all the way in the taxi there. I just cried all the time.

Eventually I knew I had to see the doctor. I told him I didn't want to be glued together with pills but he told me, 'You have to have pills to make you sleep so that you can be rested enough to try to work out what your problems are.' He gave me anti-depressants and told me I should go to see a professional. A week later when I went to see him he had made an appointment for me to see a therapist – but not for a week. I got outside and collapsed into tears on the doorstep. That was when he sent me full-speed to a nursing home.

A psychiatrist came to see me the next day and he was wonderful. I poured everything out and it was an incredible relief just to talk. My biggest problem was that I was in a disastrous relationship with a guy I'd been in love with for a long time – and whom I'd discovered was gay. I was trying to handle it and I couldn't. When you realise you're in love with someone gay it confirms all your worst fears about yourself. You think you're unattractive and it's not something you can combat. You can compete against another woman but how can you compete against another man?

To be able to speak to somebody who could understand what I was saying was terrific.

After two weeks I was told I could go home. The shrink told me to ring him if I wanted to – but the decision had to be mine. They don't make decisions for you.

I did ring – and I wish I could say that a year later I felt terrific. But I didn't. It took eight or nine years and many ups and downs. There were phases where I went to him three times a week and would have gone every day if I could have.

Because my father died when I was twelve, I felt terrible reverberations right back to childhood whenever anyone rejected me. I'd never come to terms with the fact that he let go of the reins too soon for me, I got to a stage where I couldn't look at a Father's Day card in a shop without flinching.

My shrink was the best friend I ever had. And because you're paying for the service there is never any mis-apprehension about your relationship. What they do is help you work out your problems for yourself: a shrink never gives you an answer on anything. You ask, 'Should I go here?' or 'Should I go there?' A shrink will reply, 'Well, what do you think?' He makes you work it out. When your life collapses and you stop functioning you have to learn how to cope all over again. It's like re-learning how to walk, to cross the road, relate to people.

At my lowest, if the kettle was boiling, the doorbell rang and the phone went all at once, I'd just burst into tears. A shrink helps you put your life together again, helps you with your day-to-day problems – and you can stop at that if you like. But something inside you knows there's more to it than that. So you dig a bit deeper and go a bit further back and that is where the pain begins. You find you're sitting there sobbing and you don't know where it's coming from. At this point you might start to think: this is self-indulgent, I don't need this – life's not too bad, I'm holding down my job, I've got over that guy, I've got a new car, I don't need this any more. In fact, you've put your hand in the fire and you've held it there – and at that point you *must* continue to do so. It's very hard.

At first you have to see your shrink every week, it's a crutch you can't live without. But then you find you're cancelling appointments when other things come up. You notice you haven't been for a month, a couple of months. And eventually the months turn into years.

My psychoanalyst helped me so much that unless I talk about it, everything else I've said in this book is hypoc-risy. Without him I might easily have topped myself or ended up as an old drunk in a gutter or wound up a middle-aged spinster dressed in tweeds and brogues, fat as a pig with chocolate and food my only satisfaction in life.

I think my weight problem was all tied up with self-image, with being insecure and feeling rejected. Falling in love with a gay was just another safety net. A lot of women who have no confidence in themselves find it easy to fall for gay men. My problem was I didn't know this man was gay and I wasn't prepared to find out, to admit this was a problem. When I did find out I was torn apart.

It is one of the worst pitfalls for women – falling for a gay man is like falling in love with a sadist. Gays can torture you mentally. Some of them don't like women so when you get close they take it out on you, especially all the anger and resentment some of them have against their mothers. A lot of mental beating up and knife-twisting goes on. I just thank God I was cured of all of that.

I have no plans to marry but I'm quaking in my stilettos over a clairvoyant's prediction for me for 1990. Marriage, she said confidently, was as certain before the year's end as Fergie taking a holiday.

I said, 'Okay clever clogs, who is he?' and she was pretty clear on the details: he's no more than two years older than me, has two children, is either divorced or going to be divorced.

Well, I haven't met him yet and he doesn't sound a likely candidate. I'm quite sure the only banns I'll ever have read will be when someone stands up in a pulpit and reads out the list of pubs I've been banned from – like the Pig and Whistle and the Royal Oak. Then I'll have to stand up and ask for the Firkle and Kettle, the Dog and Garter and the Stoat and Whippet to be taken into consideration.

A sure sign that wedding bells are not for me is the new Behaving Badly Frock I'm training up: it's pink and black, very tight and low and could be outrageous. But it's still being road-tested so we'll have to report back.

Suffice to say it did me proud when I went to a sporting dinner the other night with Phil and Frances Edmonds who brought along a millionaire for me (my friends do try). He fitted exactly the job description given by the crystal-ball-gazer – incredibly handsome, divorced, charming. But before we went out, Phil said to Frances and me: if you two get drunk I'm disowning you. Talk about an open invitation to get legless. So then what did I do? I turned my back on millions and pulled a blond 28-year-old who promised to phone and never did. Old habits die hard.

So I still feel my future is as a bag lady on the corner opposite Harvey Nicks – please save all your smartest bags for me: Giorgio Armani, Katherine Hamnett, Harvey Nicks (Harrods bags are much too common).

I'll be the one in pink standing there with all my possessions till I can head for the sun again.